The Economic Process: Inquiry and Challenge

RAYMOND S. IMAN

ROBERT E. MURPHY

J. M. HODGES LEARNING CENTER
WHARTON COUNTY JUNIOR COLLEGE

The Economic Process

nquiry and Challenge

aymond S. Iman
airman, Social Studies Department, Benjamin Franklin High School, Rochester, New York

obert E. Murphy
tructor, Benjamin Franklin High School, Rochester, New York

arl H. Madden
neral Editorial Consultant

44389

ott, Foresman and Company

4

General Editorial Consultant
Carl H. Madden
Chief Economist, Chamber of Commerce of the United States

Special Education Consultant
Daniel Powell
Associate Professor, Northwestern University, Evanston, Illinois

Designer: Thomas J. Gorman
Cover illustrations by Jack Breslow

Editorial Staff
Landon Risteen, Robert K. Long, Alice Kay, Barbara Ballard,
Alan Kimmel, Elizabeth Rand

Production Staff
Philip O'Neil, Irene Reilly

Copyright © 1969 by Scott, Foresman and Company, Glenview, Illinois 60025.
All Rights Reserved. Printed in the United States of America. Regional
offices of Scott, Foresman and Company are located in Atlanta, Dallas,
Glenview, Palo Alto, and Oakland, N.J.

Library of Congress Catalog Card Number 69-11212

338.973
Im1e
44389

TABLE OF CONTENTS

INTRODUCTION

The men who wrote the articles in this book often disagree with each other—sometimes violently. On the other hand, they often agree with each other—sometimes heartily. They are businessmen, labor leaders, politicians, political scientists, economists, reporters, nutritionists, and doctors. And they have all written about the same subject—economics. The ideas they have expressed and the plans they have proposed are important now. Today they are proposals; tomorrow they might help create a better world.

How, you ask, can men who disagree—and violently at that —help create a better world in which to live? How can controversy lead to understanding? The answer is that debate helps identify problems and clarify issues. Remember that the authors of these readings agree on basic economic *principles*; controversy arises over the *application* of these principles to particular problems.

You will need to understand the areas of agreement—the principles of economics—before you consider the controversies raised in *Inquiry and Challenge*. Your economics text was designed to acquaint you with these principles. *Inquiry and Challenge* was written as a supplement to *The Economic Process*, a text by Marion R. Daugherty and Carl H. Madden. It is, however, equally useful with other texts.

Nine of the twelve chapters in *Inquiry and Challenge* deal with domestic problems and two deal with international problems. Chapter 1, however, is unique. It investigates the nature of economics as well as a specific problem. You should discuss the specific problem after reading the chapter, but you should also think about the nature of economics after you have read all the other chapters.

Each chapter contains readings and questions which will help you think about the issue raised by the chapter title. The questions that precede each reading will help you pick out important material. The questions that conclude each chapter will guide you in relating ideas discussed in the readings and in supporting your answers to the title questions. You might want to prepare answers to the concluding questions before the materials are discussed in class.

Using basic principles in the investigation of economic conflict, you will find that economics does more than describe events of the past—it also supports opinions on plans for the future. You will discover that policy is made by men who are trained in a number of fields, not just by economists. Controversy brings issues into the open, where political scientists, sociologists, lawyers, and others can contribute to a just solution.

Influencing policy in cooperation with a number of other people is not an easy task. As there are few "right answers" in economics, glib predictions and highly personalized answers to complex economic problems are not valid in shaping policy.

You will also discover that economics answers the changing needs of society through controversy. Knowing that economics has gone through major changes in the past, you may conclude that it is going through a major change now. If this is the case, controversy—and a new generation of people who are not afraid of controversy—will serve its development.

Raymond S. Iman   Robert E. Murphy

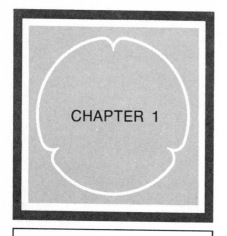

CHAPTER 1

IS ECONOMICS STILL A DISMAL SCIENCE?

Thomas Robert Malthus (English economist, 1766-1834) thought that mankind was doomed to suffer from hunger and want in the face of increasing population and insufficient resources. Upon reading Malthus' theory, Thomas Carlyle (English philosopher, 1795-1881) called economics "the dismal science". Certainly pessimistic in its prospect for mankind, the economics of Malthus was dismal in another sense, too. Because it reflected the prevailing belief in unalterable natural laws and the scarcity of goods, the study of economics was fatalistic.

Economics seemed less dismal, less fatalistic, after John Stuart Mill (English economist, 1806-1873) argued that, while the laws of production do not change, the laws of distribution can be changed. Mill's statement showed that society could take initiative in determining how to distribute wealth. Since then, economists have increasingly influenced policy making. During the Great Depression of the 1930's economists urged that the United States adopt programs to restore economic well-being. The federal government followed this urging, and now there are few groups that challenge its ability and right to maintain balance in the national economy.

Economists today are debating the extent to which government should be involved. Furthermore, they are arguing their points on the basis of the government's ability to use economics in solving current problems. What is the best way to alleviate poverty, guarantee racial equality, prolong prosperity, fight unemployment, minimize inflation, and promote public welfare?

Does this debate reflect a lack of confidence in economics and/or government to solve our modern problems? Or does it indicate that economics is changing to meet current and future needs?

The readings in this chapter are not concerned with specific current problems. On the contrary, they deal quite generally with the matter of government involvement in the national economy. While they will give you a background for debating whether or not economics is still a dismal science, they are not specific enough to allow you to come to any conclusion. The eleven chapters that follow will give you that kind of information.

Read and think about this chapter now, but give it major consideration only after you have read the other eleven chapters.

The first selection, by economist John Kenneth Galbraith, is taken from a lecture given in 1954 and published a year later. It outlines the nature of current economic controversy.

The second reading, by John E. Maher, senior economist at the Joint Council of Economic Education, pleads for a scientific approach to economic problems. In this article, published in April 1966, he points out that economics should not be considered a matter of opinion.

"The New Confusion", by Alfred L. Malabre, Jr., staff reporter for the *Wall Street Journal,* appeared in that paper in November 1967. It discusses the disagreement over whether or not government regulation of the economy contributes to inflation.

The fourth article is by Maurice H. Stans, investment banker and director of the U.S. budget under President Dwight D. Eisenhower. Appearing in December 1965, the article is an attack on the "new economics". Reflecting the thinking of English economist John Maynard Keynes (1883-1946), the new economics resulted in greater government involvement in the economy in an effort to end the Great Depression. Stans argues that, while government involvement in the economy has shown temporary success, it may have disastrous results over the long run.

The last article is by Paul A. Samuelson, professor of economics at the Massachusetts Institute of Technology. Excerpted from the seventh (1967) edition of Samuelson's widely read college economics text, this selection discusses the way economic policy and economic principles affect government action.

**ECONOMICS AND THE
ART OF CONTROVERSY**

Abridgment of "The General Economics of Argument" by John Kenneth Galbraith from ECONOMICS AND THE ART OF CONTROVERSY. Reprinted by permission of Rutgers University Press.

1 How does Galbraith define "automaticity"?
2 Under what economic conditions would an opponent of automaticity support an increase in taxes? a reduction in taxes?
3 Under what economic conditions would a supporter of automaticity oppose a budget deficit? favor an increase in taxes?
4 According to Galbraith, is economic disagreement increasing or decreasing? What evidence does he give to support his conclusion?

Should this essay, by some mischance, fall into the hands of obtuse or evil persons, it could easily be misconstrued. Such persons could have me insisting that all economic debate has now come to an end and that a reign of sweetness has replaced the bickering [and] . . . nose-punching . . . of another day. Nothing could be farther from my meaning. The capacity of economics to provoke argument seems to me still strong. No doubt there will be as much controversy over economic questions in the future as in the past, and economists should find this encouraging, for much of their income, as well as most of their prestige, derives from the persistent tendency of people to get exercised over this subject.

If there is some serious economic misfortune in the near future—for example, a disagreeable depression—the argument over what to do, and how much, and when to do it will probably become quite uncouth. This will be certain if anyone comes up with a new idea on depression therapy. As it happens, there have been no new ideas on this subject now for nearly twenty years.

The argument of these pages, rather, is that the present topics of economic controversy have seen their best days. Even this does not mean that there has been any diminution in the noise of battle. Where the art of controversy is well developed, as with us, a very small amount of substance will sustain a very great deal of fury. My case is only that the substance back of most of our current economic arguments is, indeed, rather slight. . . .

There are two questions concerning the broad structure and government of our economy which have been subjects of acute controversy in the last twenty-five years. The first and in some respects the least understood of these issues concerns the extent to which capitalism can be counted upon to turn in a reliable performance if left to itself. . . . The second controversy is over the more familiar problem of the proper scope of government activities, and particularly those activities which have come to be identified with what is called the Welfare State.

The first of these disagreements seems rather straightforward. In one view the American economy in peacetime works automatically. In the other view, it is held to require careful and at times comprehensive guidance by the government. The common test of performance here is the capacity of the economy to maintain something close to full employment. In the first view, the economy if left to itself may not offer employment to all willing workers at all times and under all peacetime circumstances. But it will come close. And it will provide more employment with less. . . damage to the freedom, moral stamina, or long-run economic well-being of the population than if the government tries to do something about it. There is a basic presumption in this view that the long-run consequences of any government action are intrinsically bad.

In the second view there is no reason to assume automatic good performance from the American economy. Left to itself, the economy will, on frequent occasions, leave willing men without work, and the production of goods that is lost during these periods of depression (or even stagnation) is lost forever. The unmanaged economy may also commit itself to bouts of serious and possibly prolonged inflation—periods when prices rise senselessly and with serious hardship to those in the community whose incomes or assets do not rise in keeping with the price advance. The counterpart of this view is the conviction that the government can do something about it. Strong and effective guidance of the economy by the government will insure good performance.

Obviously this is a formidable difference of opinion. However, the real sources of the dispute over this issue lie yet deeper. They are identified with the considerable consequences for social attitude and action which come from accepting the one view of the economy or the other. Specifically, if the economy is viewed as essentially automatic in its behavior, government in the modern state can be relatively simple and inconsequential. . . .

When the assumption of automatic good performance in the economy is denied, and when the need for government guidance of the economy is conceded, these comfortable and comprehensible standards of what government should be like no longer hold. Government is no longer simple, nor is it likely that it can be very small. . . .

Thus public works, housing, power development, reclamation, are no longer. . . justified by the desire of the people for these things and their willingness to pay for them or to have their well-to-do neighbors do so. The critical question is now the effect of these activities on production and employment and prices in the economy at large. . . .

The old tests of fiscal sanity and morality also no longer hold. When depression threatens, income should not cover outgo and a deficit is a mark of fiscal wisdom and virtue. At other times, needed public functions and services must be foregone, unneeded taxes must be levied, and a redundant surplus must be accumulated in order to check inflation. . . .

These are only a few of the complexities which are introduced when the notion of automaticity is abandoned. . . . In the physical sciences we take for granted that the intricacies of the phenomena involved will, at any early stage, pass beyond the comprehension of the ordinary man. But in the region of social phenomena we still insist on simplicity. Problems of economics and government were meant to yield to straightforward, plain common sense, and if they don't they should. . . .

But more than simple and comprehensible government is at stake in the issue of automaticity as against the guided economy. A whole new standard of public ethics is also involved. Policies which once were advanced on humanitarian and egalitarian grounds become functional. It is readily shown that they make the economy work better. Things that once were honest special privilege become damaging to the public. . . .

Here, then, is the issue. One group of controversialists has sensed the dangers of depression (and, though with infinitely less alarm, also of inflation) if the economy is left to itself. This group has gone on to the conclusion that the government must act to insure good economic performance. . . . The government intervention required, they also hold, is not too uncomfortable—it is "the kind of planning which interferes a minimum with the underpinnings of capitalism . . . ." In the main it consists of manipulation of the interest rate and of the tax and expenditure policies of the federal government. None of this implies any overt intervention in the decisions of the individual businessman. He is guided to decisions that are in keeping with good performance by the economy by indirect pressures that are indistinguishable, in general, from those of the free market.

In opposition to this sanguine view are those who have seen, or at least sensed, the dangers of abandoning the notion of automaticity which is implicit in all the above. They have seen that the notion of a guided economy is a Pandora's box filled with all sorts of political discomforts and social disciplines. They have not, accordingly, welcomed the ideas of those who have sought remedies for the instability of capitalism and in so doing have rejected the notion of automaticity. This is the chief reason for the suspicion which has come to surround the name of John Maynard Keynes in modern times. Though he was a strenuous advocate of the measures by which full employment might be achieved—and by which presumably the reputation of capitalism for performance might be saved—he also led the attack on the idea that the modern capitalist economy found its equilibrium at full employment. To many conservatives this made him as inimical a figure as Marx.

**ECONOMICS:
CONCEPTIONS
AND MISCONCEPTIONS**

Abridgment of "Economics: Conceptions and Misconceptions" by Dr. John E. Maher from SOCIAL EDUCATION (April 1966). Reprinted by permission of the author and National Council for the Social Studies. Article in WHAT IS ECONOMICS? by Dr. John E. Maher, published in 1969 by John Wiley & Sons.

1 How does Maher support the conclusion that economics is not a matter of opinion?
2 What is his definition of "economic rationalization"? How does he use the term to defend his position?

A commuter to Manhattan pays his fare and boards the 7:10 train from Chappaqua, a 90-minute ride to Grand Central. To the sociologist, this little event may symbolize the great removal of people to residences far from their places of work, and a profound change in cosmopolitan culture. . . . The economist may be struck by the special importance of maintaining passenger rail service in the face of relatively declining passenger revenues and rising costs and the severe competition between rail transportation, busses, and private passenger automobiles. . . .

The economic view of reality sees in human behavior the need to cope with the problem of resources that are scarce in relation to the objectives that they may be used to attain. . . . Thus arises the economic problem: how to allocate our scarce resources as best to satisfy our wants. Whether we are studying primitive man or the economy of a modern Western state, a monastic order or a business enterprise, an individual or a nation, the fact of scarcity pervades and conditions human behavior. . . .

. . . [Economics] may come to be thought of as international trade, money and banking, business cycles, labor relations, and a host of other areas of applications. But this, of course, is not economics. This is not what makes it a peculiar mode of inquiry of the discipline, nor does it reveal its essential structure. . . .

Our illustration of the commuter boarding a train shows that human behavior exhibits simultaneously economic, . . . sociological, and other aspects. It is not an event or a fact that is peculiarly economic, but the angle from which this fact or event is viewed. Economics is a way of organizing observations. This notion carries with it the implication that there are generally not such things as economic institutions or organizations, but rather there are institutions and organizations which, when viewed from a certain angle, display an economic aspect. Thus, neither the AFL-CIO nor the National Association of Manufacturers is solely a political, economic, or social organization, but all of these things together.

. . . Equally dangerous to sound thinking in economics is the view that economics is a matter of opinion. Some would defend this spurious notion by saying that if economics were not a matter of opinion, all economists would agree among themselves and there would be no dispute over economic policy.

Disputes, of course, do not signify the extent or nature of agreement of basic principles. Medicine, for example, is usually considered both an art and a science. No one would think of arguing that the scientific basis of medicine is questionable because different doctors are sometimes required to consult on a given case. Consultation and disagreement may arise in economics, as in medicine, because different interpretations are placed on facts, because different objectives are sought by practitioners, or because, while there is agreement on facts and on objectives, there remains contention over the appropriate methods to be used for achieving the best results. Furthermore, differences of opinion over methods may arise, not because of any disagreement on principles, but rather because certain methods entail consequences that one group finds acceptable and another finds objectionable.

The view of economics as a matter of opinion is largely fostered by those who are ignorant of the subject. Their reasons for promoting this view may be innocent or, on the contrary, may be an attempt to persuade the public of political views that are, in fact, without economic foundation. . . . If you wish in simplistic fashion to argue for the abolition of private property, or the banking system, or the public schools, then you will, indeed, require an unscientific argument. If the simplistic argument is largely based upon economics, it will have to be bad economics. And the only time a bad economic argument can be successfully advanced among any but the most economically illiterate is when it is forcefully coupled with the spurious notion that, after all, economics is only a matter of opinion. . . .

Of course, economics is not a matter of opinion. . . . [It] is true that economic "rationalization" may be offered by economists according to their own interests. But this is no different from the behavior of engineers, chemists, and others who bespeak different philosophies depending in part, upon their outlook and position in society. In no case, however, need one call into question the underlying principles that unify each of the sciences.

THE NEW CONFUSION

"The New Confusion" by Alfred L. Malabre from THE WALL STREET JOURNAL, November 17, 1967.

1 Does Malabre think that a person's psychological reaction to high prices can contribute to inflation? Why or why not?
2 How does he think that a tax increase can contribute to inflation?

Easy money means lower interest rates. Or does it mean higher interest rates? Tight money means higher interest rates. Or does it mean lower interest rates? A tax increase will stem inflation. Or will it intensify inflation?

As if today's economic situation weren't murky enough, doubts about some traditional economic concepts are proliferating.

The "new economics" of the early boom years has been supplanted, to a considerable extent, by a new uncertainty. This uncertainty is most apparent in academic circles. But it isn't going unnoticed within the perplexed ranks of public and private policy-makers. . . .

Traditionally, it has been presumed that policies that sharply increase the nation's money supply—checking accounts and currency —also tend to bring down interest rates. The logic seems plain enough: More money becomes available, so money costs borrowers less.

In some recent months, the nation's money supply has been increasing . . . faster than at any time since World War II. Overall, the January-through-October increase works out to 7.8% annually, nearly four times the average yearly rise of 2.1% during 1950-60. In absolute terms, the nation's money supply now exceeds $180 billion, more than $20 billion higher than only three years ago.

So where are interest rates? Generally, at the highest levels since the post-Civil War era. . . .

Do today's lofty interest rates mean the fast-growing money supply hasn't been growing fast enough? Or has easy money brought on the high rates?

Most Washington economic planners still adhere to the view that easy money tends to reduce interest levels. A reasonably typical view is provided by Andrew F. Brimmer, a governor of the Federal Reserve Board and a member of its Open Market Committee, which, in effect, regulates the growth of the nation's money supply. "Where the heck would interest rates be now if we hadn't been easy?" . . . . "Through the roof, that's where."

But an increasing number of authorities hold a different view. A. James Meigs, a vice president of New York's First National City Bank, says: "An increase in money-supply growth does tend to reduce interest rates at first, but then it tends to raise them later on."

This view stems from an awareness that a rapidly rising money supply ultimately increases the amounts that people earn and spend. This, in turn, tends to drive up prices in general—and specifically the price of money interest rates. . . .

A corollary to this concept is the conviction that an inflationary psychology develops, so that attempts to raise prices and interest charges meet less resistance; borrowers, for instance, balk less at paying high rates because they feel repayments will be made in cheapened dollars. . . .

Few observers go so far as to liken the present U.S. situation to that prevailing in such lands as Brazil, where the money supply grows at an annual rate of more than 33% and interest charges range as high as 60% annually on loans extending over no more than a single year.

Still, many other economists agree . . . that something akin to the banana republic atmosphere may be developing here.

Milton Friedman, a professor of economics at the University of Chicago, is perhaps the most widely recognized advocate of greater monetary restraint. Mr. Friedman, a consultant to the Federal Reserve Board, appears convinced that "over the long run, acceleration of monetary growth raises interest rates." . . .

No statistics pinpoint how widely Mr. Friedman's ideas about the economic role of money pervade the economics community. But Paul W. McCracken, a former member of the President's Council of Economic Advisers and now a professor at the University of Michigan, declares that "More of us are becoming Friedmanites." And Homer Jones of the St. Louis Fed [Federal Reserve Board] recently estimated that perhaps one of every three economists now adheres to Friedman-style monetary ideas.

The present division of economic opinion is by no means limited to the monetary area. Most business analysts still believe a tax increase, such as the 10% surcharge recently proposed by President Johnson [enacted in 1968], would help to curtail price and credit inflation. But this view is certainly not unanimous.

Thomas B. Curtis, a Republican Congressman from Missouri and a member of the House Ways and Means Committee that has held up the tax proposal, flatly says that the Administration would "intensify inflation" rather than reduce it.

Such opinion appears based on a variety of considerations.

Congressman Curtis, among others, stresses that the sort of price inflation that the country currently suffers is essentially a reflection of fast-rising costs. In such a situation, the proposed tax increase would simply add to the cost pressure, and ultimately to price inflation, as companies (through price increases) and individuals (through higher wages) attempt to pass on any new tax "cost."

Some analysts further suggest that the tax proposal would tend simply to reduce the currently high rate of personal savings, rather than trim consumer spending, as planned. Recently, perhaps in anticipation of a tax boost, savings have averaged roughly 7% of consumers' after tax income. Through most of the past decade, in contrast, this savings rate has been well under 5%.

A reduction in savings to pay for higher taxes, some economists say, would tend to drain investment funds from various thrift institutions, such as savings and loan associations. Such a development, it's argued, would only add to the inflationary strains already evident in financial markets. These markets would be further strained, some analysts contend, if a tax boost also prompted corporations to borrow more heavily to pay for capital expenditures that otherwise would have been financed out of higher after-tax earnings.

THE OTHER SIDE OF THE "NEW ECONOMICS"

By Maurice H. Stans. Reprinted from *U. S. News & World Report* (December 13, 1965). Copyright 1965. U. S. News & World Report, Inc.

1 Why is Stans critical of the new economics?
2 How does he answer the contention that the new economics has functioned successfully in the last decade?

We are witnessing in Washington a daring attempt to devise new concepts for a solution of the persistent problem of the uneven distribution of the national wealth and output.

There is, in fact, under way in our seat of Government the biggest economic experiment the world has ever seen. It is important that each of us understand clearly what it is and what it seeks to achieve, and what risks are involved, for our personal fortunes and our national future are at stake on the outcome.

The national economic policy which is now so aggressively being tested is not designed as a temporary expedient to meet a momentary difficulty. It is an avowed way of life.

If it succeeds, it will be a major turning point in the economics of government. Historians will record it as a complete reversal in direction for the science of political management.

If it fails, it will be an equally historic event that may forever shatter the strength of our free democratic processes.

These wide-scale economic experiments are the brain children of a present generation of liberal economists holding considerable influence in Government affairs. They do not comprise a compact group, and their ideas are not uniform, but in general they endorse and support these propositions of governmental economics:

1. That a Government can spend a nation into prosperity and assure full employment of its manpower and resources—by a process of force-feeding the economy through planned deficits;

2. That a limited amount of inflation is good for the country —or, at least, does no harm;

3. That a tax cut, when a deficit exists, will stimulate the economy and thereby enhance total revenues—enough to achieve future surpluses;

4. That the national debt need never be reduced—and should, in fact, be increased as the national output grows. . . .

In short, government should intervene more in economic planning and management. Only then can we gain a satisfactory annual rate of growth and a suitable level of living.

All this is usually described as the "new economics." To the advocates of these precepts, anything else is an incantation from the forgotten past, an ancient cliché, a worn-out tradition. There are immediate questions that these propositions bring to mind:

Can a government successfully cast out the long-accepted tenet that, to be financially strong, it must live within its income?

Will persistent deficit spending really provide enough steam to iron out the wrinkles and gaps in employment of manpower and resources?

To what extent and for how long can annual deficits be suffered and national debt be accumulated without imposing severe inflation, with its consequent loss of values and of security, especially harsh for those on fixed incomes?

Can a small degree of inflation be encouraged without serious risk that it will get out of control?

As part of all this, how safe is it for government to offer its people the attractive carrot of recurring tax reductions when there is already an existing substantial gap between revenues and expenses?

If the "new economics" succeeds, it would without a doubt create a new era for the United States and, in fact, for the entire community of nations. Never again would a national government need to be inhibited in the scope of its services to the people by old-fashioned thinking. Central economic planning would become a major tool of progress . . . .

It may be boldness even to question these policies when, after a few years, they already seem to be highly successful. But a few years of success do not insure their long-time survival in the face of the inevitable pressures of a democratic society, and it is over the long term that their ultimate value will be judged. . . .

Certainly . . . there are grounds for skepticism about the optimistic and confident assurances of the liberal economists. . . . Perhaps among the long-term risks of the "new economics" in the United States are these:

1. The risk of failure—with a high penalty in accumulated debt, loss of value of our currency, disastrous inflation, and loss of our position of world leadership.

2. The risk of success—which might, paradoxically, bring about another epidemic of failures in weaker nations tempted by the sweet smell of our achievement, but unable to keep their programs in bounds, and might also tempt us to demand too much of a good thing and thereby bring about our downfall.

3. The risk of degradation of the national purpose and spirit —which would be an inevitable accompaniment of a reversal of the deep-seated traditions of thrift, self-responsibility, freedom of choice, and driving ambition . . . .

4. The risk of loss of personal freedoms—a price which most likely would have to be paid for the all-powerful central government that long-range economic planning and controls would bring and high spending would create. . . .

In summary, the new economic theories have the attractions of promising much, providing a pleasant euphoria of irresponsibility and postponing the reckoning to other generations. But the evidence of experience is unanimous in showing that they cannot be sure of success. . . .

Is the "new economics" a blueprint for Utopia or a temporary mess of economic pottage?

Only history will tell, but the signs so far suggest that there are more reasons for skepticism than seem to be generally recognized.

INTRODUCTION TO ECONOMICS

Abridged from ECONOMICS: AN INTRODUCTORY ANALYSIS by Paul A. Samuelson. Copyright © 1967 by McGraw-Hill, Inc. Used by permission of McGraw-Hill Book Company.

1 How do human and social behavior contribute to disagreement among economists, according to Samuelson?
2 What distinction does Samuelson make between "economic principles" and "economic policy"?
3 Why does Samuelson think that a little knowledge is particularly dangerous in economics?

It is the first task of modern economic science to describe, to analyze, to explain, and to correlate the behavior of production, unemployment, prices, and similar phenomena. If they are to be significant, descriptions must be more than a series of disconnected narratives. They must be fitted into a systematic pattern, and this is what is meant by true analysis.

Because of the complexity of human and social behavior, we cannot hope to attain the precision of a few of the physical sciences. We cannot perform the controlled experiments of the chemist or biologist. Like the astronomer, we must be content largely to "observe." But economic events and statistical data observed are, alas, not so well behaved and orderly as the paths of heavenly satellites. Fortunately, our answers need not be accurate to several decimal places; on the contrary, if the right general *direction* of cause and effect can be determined, we shall have made a tremendous step forward. . . .

. . . Ultimately, understanding should aid in control and improvement. How can the vagaries of the business cycle be diminished? How can economic progress and efficiency be furthered? How can adequate standards of living be made more widely available?

At every point of our analysis we shall seek to shed light on these policy problems. To succeed in this, we must all try to cultivate an objective and detached ability to see things as they *are*, regardless of our likes or dislikes. The fact must be faced that economic issues are close to everybody emotionally. . . .

. . . [There] is only one valid reality in a given economic situation, however hard it may be to recognize and isolate it. There is not one theory of economics for Republicans and one for Democrats, one for workers and one for employers. On the basic economic principles concerning prices and employment, most economists are in fairly close agreement.

This statement does not mean that economists always agree in the *policy* field. . . . Basic questions concerning right and wrong goals to be pursued cannot be settled by science as such. They belong in the realm of ethics and "value judgments." The citizenry must ultimately decide such issues. What the expert can do is point out the feasible alternatives and the true costs that may be involved in the different decisions. . . .

From childhood days on, everyone knows something about economics. This acquaintance is both helpful and deceptive: helpful, because much knowledge can be taken for granted; deceptive, because it is natural and human to accept superficially plausible views. A little knowledge may be dangerous. On close examination common sense may prove to be really nonsense.

A union leader who has successfully negotiated several labor contracts may feel that he is an expert on the economics of wages. A businessman who has "met a payroll" may feel that his views on price control are final. A banker who can balance his books may conclude that he knows all there is to know about the creation of money. Each individual naturally tends to judge an economic event by its immediate effect upon himself. . . .

In an introductory survey, the economist is interested in the workings of the economy *as a whole* rather than in the viewpoint of any one group. Social and national policies rather than individual policy are his goals. . . .

The economic world is extremely complicated. As we noted, it is usually not possible to make economic observations under the controlled experimental conditions characteristic of scientific laboratories. . . . If . . . [the economist] wishes to determine the effect of a gasoline tax on fuel consumption, he may be vexed by the fact that, in the same year when the tax was imposed, pipelines were first introduced. Nevertheless, he must try—if only mentally—to isolate the effects of the tax, "other things being equal." Otherwise, he will understand the economic effects neither of taxation nor of transportation improvements, nor of both together.

The difficulty of analyzing causes when controlled experimentation is impossible is well illustrated by the confusion of the savage medicine man who thinks that both witchcraft and a little arsenic are necessary to kill his enemy, or that only after he has put on a green robe in spring will the trees do the same. As a result of this limitation and many others, our quantitative economic knowledge is far from complete. This does not mean that we do not have great amounts of accurate statistical knowledge available. We do. Reams of census data, market information, and financial statistics have been collected by governments, trade associations, and business concerns.

Even if we had more and better data, it would still be necessary—as in every science—to *simplify*, to *abstract* from the infinite mass of detail. No mind can comprehend a bundle of unrelated facts. All analysis involves abstraction. It is always necessary to *idealize*, to omit detail, to set up simple hypotheses and patterns by which the facts can be related, to set up the right questions before going out to look at the world as it is. Every theory, whether in the physical or biological or social sciences, distorts reality in that it oversimplifies. But if it is good theory, what is omitted is outweighed by the beam of illumination and understanding that is thrown over the diverse empirical data.

Properly understood, therefore, theory and observation, deduction and induction, cannot be in conflict. . . . Consequently, when a student says, "That's all right in theory but not in practice," he really means, "That's not all right in the relevant theory," or else he is talking nonsense.

Particularly in the social sciences, we must watch out for the "tyranny of words." The world is complicated enough without introducing further confusions and ambiguities because (1) two different names are unknowingly being used for the same thing or (2) the same one word is being applied to two quite different phenomena.

Jones may call Robinson a liar for holding that the cause of depression is oversaving, saying, "Underconsumption is really the cause." Schwartz may enter the argument, asserting, "You are both wrong. The real trouble is underinvestment." They may go on arguing; but if they really stopped to analyze their language, they might find that there were no differences in their opinions about the facts and that only a verbal confusion was involved. . . . One does not have to be an expert in *semantics*—the study of language and its meaning—to realize that scientific discussion requires us to avoid such emotional terminology wherever possible.

QUESTIONS FOR CLOSER STUDY

1 Are economic principles more influential than economic policy in the solution of national economic problems? Why or why not?

2 Between which of the following pairs of writers is there *most agreement*? (a) Malabre and Galbraith, (b) Maher and Stans, (c) Samuelson and Galbraith. Support your conclusion.

3 Would Stans support or reject the theory of automaticity? Why?

4 On the basis of the evidence in *all* the readings, do you think that economics is a matter of opinion? Why or why not?

5 Do you think that economics is "dismal" in the sense that it is pessimistic? Why or why not?

6 Do you think that it should and/or could be in the realm of economics to alleviate poverty, guarantee racial equality, prolong prosperity, fight unemployment, minimize inflation, and promote public welfare? Why or why not?

CHAPTER 2

IS THE CONSUMER
PAWN OR KING?

The economy of the United States is the most productive the world has ever seen. Most Americans share in this prosperity. Indeed, by world standards even our poor are well off.

It has been said that within this economy the consumer is supreme. By his exercise of free choice in the market place, he decides what goods and services are to be made available, how many are made available, and how much they shall cost. At first glance the theory seems unassailable.

But there are dissenters who question that the consumer actually exercises free choice. They wonder, for example, why many American men who work at office jobs, who are overweight and in dire need of exercise, should mow their lawns sitting down. They wonder why a family should trade in a perfectly good automobile for a new one, no more functional than the other. Why should a family own three television sets, six radios, a boat used twice a year, and have closets full of little-worn clothing? Does the consumer make these buying decisions for himself or is he the victim of the pressures of a high-production economy?

The critics point to the subtle influences producers use to

sell products. Psychologists, for example, have studied the effect of color on the consumer's subconscious, or how the desire for status may cause the buyer to choose one product over another. The critics argue that experts study packaging as a way of influencing or even deceiving the consumer. Finally, they view with suspicion the whole field of advertising. Does advertising inform or does it appeal mostly to the emotions? How much does it add to the cost of the product?

In recent years producers have been moving away from the policy of *caveat emptor* (let the buyer beware) and toward *caveat venditor* (let the seller beware), thus placing more and more responsibility for quality goods in the hands of the seller. And by 1968 Congress either had passed or was considering a number of bills in the area of consumer protection. However, there has been little comparable change in advertising policies, and the controversy in this area continues.

The chapter begins with a selection written in 1963 by Marion Harper, Jr., a former chairman of Interpublic, Inc., parent company of many advertising agencies. As a marketing executive he defends America's high-level production and argues that increased consumption is the key to economic growth.

The author of the second reading is Robert Theobald, a well-known economist and writer. Writing in 1961, Theobald deplores the methods producers use to increase sales in what he terms an overproducing society.

The third and fourth selections appeared in a 1962 issue of a professional marketing journal. The former is by Thomas A. Petit,

professor of business administration, and Alan Zakon, then a teacher
of marketing. It contends that advertising is a bulwark to existing
values in this country. The latter is by Colston E. Warne, professor
of economics and active spokesman for consumers for many years.
It is a criticism, not only of advertising, but also of other selling practices the author thinks are unethical.

**TOO RICH, TOO SOFT,
TOO SURFEITED?**

Abridged from "Too Rich, Too Soft,
Too Surfeited?" by Marion Harper,
Jr. from SATURDAY REVIEW (April
13, 1963). Reprinted by permission of
the author and Saturday Review.

1 How does the author interpret the term "saturated"?
2 How does he reply to the accusation that American markets are saturated?
3 What proof does he offer to support the contention that the consumer influences
what is produced? Is the proof convincing?
4 What benefits, beyond satisfaction of material needs, does the author claim for
the American economy?

Producers and marketers of the nation's consumer goods
today face some perplexing contradictions in the advice offered by
critics and well-wishers, both in and out of government.

On the one hand, they are urged on to more prodigious
effort, to greater and greater productivity, as a means of advancing
national growth and improving the lot of needier nations. On the
other, they are warned . . . that they have gone far enough—too
far, in fact; that they have "saturated" the market with goods that
people don't need, and through subtle persuasion are forcing more
and more unneeded things all the time. . . .

Studying the admitted paradoxes—a lagging national growth
rate in the midst of unprecedented production, a stubborn level of
unemployment in a time of record employment, a standard of living
that daily appears in more dramatic contrast to that of most of the
world—we should perhaps ask these questions:

From the sociologist's point of view, has our standard of
living soared beyond what is "good" for us? From the economist's

point of view, has it reached a ceiling? . . .

These questions, and their answers, bear not only on the future direction of American society, but on our relations with the rest of the world.

It has become an emblem of chic to bewail U.S. affluence as something somehow evil, or at least suspect. Perhaps because we ourselves are inheritors of a Puritan tradition that equates austerity with virtue and comfort with wickedness, we are quick to hang our heads over material success, and to . . . renounce the world and, like St. Francis, give our all to the poor.

But before such renunciation, and with rather more contemporary concern for the poor, it might be wise to examine the reasons for our embarrassment of riches. It's possible that affluence isn't all that bad. . . .

Except during wars, we have always taken as our economic goal the improvement of living standards. Consumers, within the limits of their purses, have always decided what those living standards should be. . . .

Normally, consumers purchase over two-thirds of our national output of goods and services—three-fourths, if we add housing. Through their purchase of products, they also shape our industrial capacity. Business invests in plant and equipment largely on the basis of consumer demand. . . .

What early distinguished the United States from other industrial nations was not economic methods or resources, but their extraordinary development in a world without rigid social traditions. The patronage of the few was transformed into the buying power of the many, as extremes of aristocracy and poverty merged into an expanding middle class. This 200-year experiment in "middle-classless" society, with its unprecedented social and economic mobility, undoubtedly deserves chief credit for our present living standards.

But have we mined this vein—of consumer economy—too long? Are our people too rich, too soft, too surfeited with goods? Before making final judgments let us review the evidence.

First, consider the purely economic notion of "saturation." Are American markets literally saturated? What markets? At what income levels?

Too many houses, perhaps? The American home market is

"saturated" in the sense that almost every family has a roof over its head. But the latest census [1960] records that nearly a fifth of all U.S. dwellings are "dilapidated or lacking one or more plumbing facilities." That's nearly four out of twenty.

We are building dwellings at the rate of 1,400,000 a year. But we are adding *households* at the rate of 900,000 a year. That means we have only 500,000 houses available for upgrading the supply. And by the early 1970s the rate of family formation will have almost doubled.

Or, too many cars? True, ownership is widely distributed: Nine out of ten families with incomes over $5,000 have a car. Yet a surprisingly large proportion of American families—about 22 per cent—are without a car.

About 5,000,000 automobiles are scrapped every year because they no longer have value as transportation. But almost 900,000 households are formed each year. Simply to maintain our present level of ownership, we would need almost 6,000,000 new cars a year.

Further, one of every three cars on the road is eight years old or older; and many should be replaced for reasons of safety, apart from performance.

In a country as dependent on individual transportation as ours is, with three carless families out of ten, and another three with relics of years ago, we can hardly have a finding of "saturation."

We are often described as the happy slaves of mechanical appliances. But ownership of these conveniences is by no means universal. Only one in twelve American families has a dishwasher, only one in five an air conditioner.

Moreover, our present supply of such appliances is being exhausted in use at a rate almost equal to all current production. We are thus faced with a replacement demand, as well as the potential of a latent market.

Again, the label of "saturation" is inaccurate in economic terms. As used currently, the word is often charged with emctional powder, and usually represents a value judgment of the commentator. A sewing machine, an air conditioner, a clothes washer, an automobile may be one person's "saturation" and another's freedom from drudgery, and opportunity for study, recreation, or travel.

Much criticism of our consumer-goods abundance can be

summed up in expressions like "things people don't need," or . . . "material goods that we should never have dreamed of wanting had we been left to ourselves." But who is to say what people "need" beyond the means of survival? Most of the good things of civilization have not been necessities—universities, for example.

The prophet of "saturation" ignores the reality of a new world. It would seem that some time ago he should have put his foot down against the stove, tap water, printing, antibiotics, lipstick, and possibly the wheel. But he didn't; and now in shouting "enough" he is implicitly calling not only for a freeze in the production of goods, but in the living standards of highly mobile income groups. . . .

It is still the consumer, in our society, who determines what is "enough" or "too much." This of course runs counter to the stereotype of a docile public, subject to the hypnotizing powers of advertising, and an easy mark for every new product inducement. Any practitioner of mass persuasion can testify that consumers show remarkable resistance to products that are not to their liking. Advertising and publicity failed to sell the sack dress or the Edsel; and much more massive promotion apparently fails to persuade East Germans that they have inherited the earth. . . .

But the critical question remains: Is our consumer-goods economy a force of decadence? Is it a hindrance to desirable goals of maintaining peace, educating the young, creating full employment, or conserving our natural resources?

It should be remembered that no economy can be praised or blamed outside its competence, which is to perform well and equitably in providing for the material welfare of its adherents. . . . If it functions well, it may help free its supporters to make the best use of their talents, and provide an environment in which philosophers, teachers, artists, and statesmen can flourish.

Our present economy—of abundance with some waste, of affluence with some vulgarity—has enabled us to give help and hope to many nations beyond our boundaries; to provide the chief support for international peace efforts; to create and sustain the revolutionary idea of universal education; to make history's most successful assault on poverty and disease.

That is not enough to satisfy us; but it is substantial—and

34

perhaps sufficient, for the moment, to justify an economy based on the principle of more for everybody—with everybody having a vote in what it produces and provides.

**ABUNDANCE—
THREAT OR PROMISE?**

From CHALLENGE OF ABUNDANCE by Robert Theobald. © 1961 by Robert Theobald. Used by permission of Clarkson N. Potter, Inc.

1 What does the author mean by "consumer seduction"? Is it a loaded term?
2 In what ways may advertising be an assault on privacy?
3 How may packaging be used to deceive the consumer?
4 Why should the United States Steel Corporation be interested in how much is spent on packaging?
5 Why is it claimed that increasing amounts of money will be spent on advertising to attract teen-agers?

Any business, in the accepted use of the term, *must* make a profit if it is to survive: stated this way, it appears a logical and obvious thought. However, discussion of the *implications* of this drive for profit is hampered by a lack of suitable descriptive terms. We have never developed, for instance, a word to include all individuals and institutions producing goods and services for profit. For present purposes, it is necessary to identify two important elements in the market picture by allocating to each of them a descriptive term. Thus, a "marketive" will be employed to describe any organization or individual producing goods and/or services in an attempt to make a monetary profit, and an "ecofact" will be employed to describe any of these goods and services. . . .

Marketives . . . have increasingly felt compelled to strengthen their efforts to persuade the consumer to buy, for they have recognized that it is *not* a lack of productive capacity which limits their output at the present time but rather their inability to sell all the ecofacts that they could produce. Rapid increases in expenditure on consumer seduction, using advertising, packaging and research and development, have therefore taken place. The rapid rise in spending on consumer seduction has been accompanied by a growing chorus of indignant, and sometimes shrill, accusations of deception and carelessness on the part of research-and-development personnel, packagers and particularly admen. The charges have been denied with equal emphasis by those accused, especially the admen, who are, after all, in the image-making business. This noisy and highly publicized exchange has obscured a far more profound dialogue now going on between two groups who, while they agree that the controversy does not primarily concern personal morality but rather social responsibility, disagree as to the effects of the ever-increasing volume of advertising.

Between 1950 and 1961-1962, the total cost of advertising as a percentage of total consumer expenditures for all ecofacts rose from 2.9 per cent to 3.6 per cent. Arno H. Johnson of the J. Walter Thompson advertising agency forecasts a further increase to about 5 per cent by 1972. Do we want to be exposed to twice as much advertising as at present? How much of existing advertising is informative and how much falls into the category of the analgesic commercial whose background music must make one suspect that it is designed to bring on the headache which the product would hopefully relieve? When are we entitled to privacy from the sales pitch? Ernest van der Haag, professor of social philosophy at New York University, has recently estimated: "On a weekday, a man and his wife, engaged in an average number of normal activities—reading the newspaper, traveling to the office and back, reading a magazine, listening to the radio, viewing TV—are exposed to between 1,500-2,000 general advertisements, not counting those in business and professional magazines, or direct mail." When considering this extensive exposure to advertising, it is perhaps not irrelevant that a recent survey reported in *Advertising Age* revealed that only 8 per cent of American admen considered that others in the profession were "honest."

A second method for increasing sales proposes greater expenditures on packaging. U.S. Steel's executive vice president has estimated that "Packaging-industry sales amount to almost $20,000,000,000 a year and may reach $30,000,000,000 within five years." . . . Already the package, narrowly defined as pack, box, etc., often costs more than the product it encloses. For example, it is now more expensive to repack soap powder, if a change in design of the box should be decided, than to throw it away. In addition, "deception" is rife in this field. Senator Maurine B. Neuberger [member of Congress, 1960-1966] has introduced legislation to curb abuses. She comments in the *Retail Clerks International Advocate*:

> If you're not going to make your package larger than it need to be to hold the ingredients, at least you can confuse the shopper by using an odd-sized container. Marketing your product in a weirdly shaped bottle is an excellent way of preventing the customer from comparing its size with a competing product. If you can flatten out your cereal box, you can make it taller and wider; if you put a narrow neck in a bottle, you can make it taller.

> But slack-filled, distorted packages are just the beginning! Science has come to the aid of the producer who wants to enlarge the apparent size of his product without adding any more of its costly ingredients. He injects water into a ham or processed cheese, or markets "balloon" bread, where a one pound loaf is baked in a one and one-half pound pan.

In addition to advertising and packaging, marketives try to increase their sales by achieving "uniqueness" for their ecofacts through research and development. Most marketives try to carve out a market for their own ecofacts by stressing some quality which is not available, or which is implied not to be available, in other similar ecofacts. They do not sell toothpaste, but "Y's superhextozed toothcleanser"; they do not simply clean clothes, but they offer "Z's special process with added L&R." In this way they hope to convince the consumer that their ecofact is so different from all others that price should be a minor, if not an irrelevant, factor in choosing between ecofacts. . . . One packaged-goods executive said: "If we've got a real product difference, we could let any kid from Harvard Business School write the ads. When we've got parity of products, though, that's when we need the pros."

. . . There appears to be a possibility that the amount spent nationally to influence the consumer may exceed the amount spent nationally on formal education. In addition, expenditures on consumer seduction will compete more and more directly with education because of the changing age structure of the population—by 1965, 50 per cent of the population will be under twenty-five. This statistic alone would cause the marketive to concentrate more attention on this group, but there will be even more encouragement to spend large quantities of money to attract teen-agers because they are likely to be particularly affected by advertising. Eugene Gilbert of the

Gilbert Marketing Group recently commented: "Teen-agers are a follow-the-leader group. They are more susceptible." . . .

Aldous Huxley sketched the results of a highly technological, over-producing, forced-consumption economy in his deeply prophetic book, *Brave New World,* although he suggested that centuries would elapse before the society he described would develop. His more recent writing, particularly *Brave New World Revisited,* shows why he now fears the development of just such an *a*human society within a very brief period of years. There is increasingly general concern among social scientists that Huxley's prophecies may indeed come true unless there is a change in the directional drives of Western society.

**ADVERTISING
AND SOCIAL VALUES**

"Advertising and Social Values" by Thomas A. Petit and Alan Zakon from JOURNAL OF MARKETING, Vol. 26 (October 1962). Reprinted by permission of the publisher, The American Marketing Association.

1 Do you agree with the authors that advertising reflects American values?
2 Are the authors concerned with advertising itself or the quality of advertising?
3 How can a society protect itself from conflicting values of another society? Should advertising be an "institution of social control"?
4 What do Petit and Zakon mean by the statement, "what a man consumes, a man is"?
5 In what ways, according to the authors, does advertising protect freedom?

A common criticism of advertising is that it violates our system of values. Advertising is charged with exalting materialism at the expense of traditional spiritual values in American life.

Historian David Potter says in *People of Plenty* that "the most important [effects] . . . of this powerful institution (advertising) are not upon the economics of our distributive system; they are upon the values of our society." Potter considers abundance to be a major force in American history and advertising to be the institution of abundance. He compares advertising with the school and church in the magnitude of its social influence; and says that it dominates the mass media, has vast power in shaping popular standards, and is one of a limited number of institutions which exercises social control. Potter's major criticism is that advertising, unlike the school and church, does not have as a goal the betterment of the individual.

Analyses of this kind usually proceed in the following way: (1) We need a high level of consumption to keep our tremendously productive economic system fully employed. (2) This requires a consumption-oriented population. (3) Advertising trains people in their role of consumer. (4) As a result of advertising, people covet material rather than spiritual values.

There is much validity to this chain of reasoning, so far as it goes. There can be no doubt that demand rather than supply, and affluence rather than scarcity, are the crux of our economic problem in America. For the first time in history a great nation has developed sufficient technological might to make it difficult for her people to maintain the pace of consumption required to keep the machines working full time. Advertising, as the social institution of persuasion *par excellence,* is bound to play an important role in such an economy.

But this does not necessarily mean that advertising subverts the American value system. This is not possible. As any copywriter can tell you, advertising must be compatible with the values of the consumer if it is to influence his behavior. Advertising is an educating and not a forcing process. It interprets the want-satisfying qualities of the product for the consumer. To do this, it must relate product characteristics and consumer benefits to values the customer has already learned. The surest way to lose a sale and a customer is to go against the tide of what people think is right and wrong.

Why, then, do so many intellectuals and moralists hold advertising in such contempt? It is because of a misunderstanding of the causal relationship between advertising and social values. . . .

We get our values from the family, play group, school, church, and other social institutions. As we grow up, these values are internalized, and we become socialized so that we can take our place in society. The function of advertising is to help socialize us so that we are prepared to play our role as consumers; and as consumers we are supposed to consume more standardized goods. It is necessary that our tastes are easily influenced and anticipated if consumption is to be sufficiently dynamic to clear the ever expanding market.

Advertising is merely a means to an end, and the end is a consumption-oriented people. Thus, the question of whether or not advertising contradicts our value system hinges on the legitimacy of high-level consumption as a social goal. . . .

The truth of the matter is that *the critics of advertising are not really criticizing advertising; they are criticizing the American value system itself.*

. . . It is the value system which determines the nature and significance of social institutions like advertising, not the other way around. The value system is the most precious possession of society. It is protected against conflicting values coming in from other societies and from internal rebellion with society by institutions of social control.

Advertising is one of these institutions. Since it is in the service of the value system, advertising cannot run counter to it and survive. On the contrary, it must protect social values. If the critics of advertising would stop confusing their ideal value systems with what the American value system really is, they would see that advertising is a bulwark rather than a threat to our existing values. . . .

There is more than a grain of truth in the saying, "What a man consumes, a man is." Therefore, advertising serves as a mediating device between the value of equality and the individual's need for a sense of identity based on social class structure.

Perhaps the best way to understand the relationship between advertising and social values is to begin with the question, "Why do we allow advertising to exist?" There are legal means to do away with it any time we wish, but very few people would approve such an action. Why? What is there about advertising that is of value in the American way of life?

The answer is to be found in perhaps the most fundamental of American values—the fear of the illegitimate use of centralized authority. This negative value probably developed as a spontaneous response of the colonies to the dependent status they were forced to occupy by England. In political life, this value has time and time again manifested itself in the voter attitude of "rotating the rascals" out of office who are now in office. It is the reason for the deep American commitment to the public policy toward power of checks and balances. In economic life, the fear of the illegitimate use of centralized power has been the mainstay of capitalism against the threat of socialism and communism. Americans prefer capitalism because it is associated in their minds and feelings with individual freedom (which is a positive way of stating the fear of illegitimate use of centralized power).

But a capitalistic system which is subject to severe depressions offers precious little freedom from the ills of an industrial civilization. Therefore, anything which helps to stabilize economic activity at a high level of employment becomes associated with individual freedom. Since advertising has as its objective the maintenance of a high level of demand, it is a freedom-protecting institution.

**ADVERTISING—
A CRITIC'S VIEW**

"Advertising—A Critic's View" by Colston E. Warne from JOURNAL OF MARKETING, Vol. 26 (October 1962). Reprinted by permission of the publisher, The American Marketing Association.

1 According to the author, "program content is rightfully not the creature of the advertiser. . . ." Since the advertiser on radio and TV is paying the bill, should he not decide program content?
2 Why does the author favor the principle of *caveat venditor* over *caveat emptor?*
3 What is the role of the nation's opinion leaders in the debate over advertising, according to Warne?
4 Is the proper role of advertising an educational one?
5 Is it possible that truth in advertising may be profitable to the seller? How?

[There is a] need for a *consumer manifesto* which would include as a minimum the acceptance of the following basic elements:

1. The new communication media—radio and television—were not created for advertising. The airwaves are owned by the consuming public; and the costs of radio and television, whether indirectly assessed through advertising or directly through the cost of electricity and television acquisition and maintenance, are consumer costs. Advertisers are there incidentally as nonpaying guests in the home and are not to be obnoxious, long-winded, stupid, or inane. Program content is rightfully not the creature of the adver-

tiser, dedicated by his dictates to cater to the lowest common denominator of mass taste.

2. The countryside belongs to the consumer, not to the advertiser. There is no inherent right to create incessant affronts to the human eye every hundred yards along a highway—a procession of billboard slums.

3. Newspapers and periodicals have their central responsibility to their readers, not to their advertisers. This responsibility is compromised whenever dubious standards of advertising acceptance prevail or where choice is warped by planted stories designed to sell, not to inform.

4. Legislative and self-regulatory efforts to impose truth in advertising and to ban false and misleading advertising, although possessed of great merit, have thus far proven notoriously ineffective. They need to be improved. No prohibitions on false advertising, however drastic, can suffice to compel advertising to play its essential role in our culture. Truth in advertising is not a residue left after the elimination of falsehood. Advertising has ever been prone to discover new techniques of subtle deception wherever prohibitions have been imposed. What is today needed is the application of a supplementary approach.

5. Specifically, a policy is proposed of *caveat venditor*—let the seller beware—a policy to be enforced by our social and legal institutions. An advertisement should be a warranty to the purchaser of the price and quality of an article. Thus, the burden of proof as to an advertising claim will lie squarely upon the seller of a branded good. A claim should be accurate and complete as to all essential details, and should constitute a full disclosure of both the merits and demerits of the good in its intended use. Advertising should not be poised on the slippery edge of irrelevance, misrepresentation, or deception. The obsolescent and socially destructive idea of *caveat emptor* [let the buyer beware] should be appropriately buried as a relic of the days of simple markets and well-understood commodities.

This suggestion that the seller be held legally bound by his statements (including the clear implications that these may give to the ordinary consumer) is by no means a revolutionary one. It has been already incorporated into a number of court opinions and is beginning to find a place in economic and judicial attitudes. It should now be fully integrated into the legal structure. Full disclosure in one form or another has already emerged in declarations of ingredients in foods and drugs; hazardous substances have to have full warnings on their labels. Moreover, the drift of court opinion has been toward the acceptance of the principle that in placing a product upon the market, the manufacturer assumes a responsibility to the consumer which goes far beyond the mandate of *caveat emptor.*

There are probably no consumers who are not willing, even eager, to be told with accuracy and candor about new or truly improved products, or for that matter to have their memories jogged about the merits of existing products. The consumer has no quarrel with advertising as such. His basic quarrel is simply that this medium has been misused. As a whole, it has not been designed to inform, but has been powered for a lesser objective—the promotion of brands. And being so powered, it has less often led to consumer enlightenment than to consumer bewilderment.

It is all very well for advertising partisans to plead that only one out of five Americans is disgusted with its actual performance and that in the main the nation is well content with the toothy blondes who greet them with beckoning hands filled with the fruits of our culture. Correct it may be that the majority of the consumer "electorate" basks contentedly in the advertising sun. But the revolt against advertising has come from opinion leaders, and the rise of American educational levels may well extend the area of alienation.

Must life be made meaningful solely by the efforts of specialists in stimulation who, in quest of self-profit, seek to coax or cajole? Has not the most important force—that of self-initiation—been omitted?

The critic of advertising does not wish to establish a standardized consumer after his own image. A discerning critic wishes more deliberative choice, more autonomous human beings who operate in an environment which, with truthful information sources, fosters freedom of choice and free competition of ideas in the marketplace—not the preconditioned "standard package" of acceptable goods of the advertiser.

It is advertising that is concentrating its techniques upon the manipulation of human personality into profitable molds. To be sure, it is no hidden persuader. It is instead a private agency of human conditioning of not inconsiderable power, designed generally to create an image of sterile optimism, an obsession with material things . . . with change . . . with motion . . . and with superficial appearance. Its failure to date has not been so much in craftsmanship as in its refusal to recognize that accurate advertising is a phase of educational experience and should maintain the standards of education. It should be fact-faithful, presenting the imperfections as well as the advantages; it should have perspective; it should be tentative and as unbiased as possible. Artificial product differentiations and romantic fantasies may for a time capture unthinking consumer loyalty; but these techniques are no substitute for unadulterated truth.

QUESTIONS FOR CLOSER STUDY

1 The articles by Harper and by Petit and Zakon both stress the positive values of advertising. Which is more convincing in showing the economic achievements and social gains brought about with the help of advertising?

2 Are Theobald and Warne attacking advertising on the same grounds?

3 Do newspapers and periodicals use public facilities in the same way as radio and television stations? Is the responsibility to the public of newspapers and magazines different from that of radio and television stations?

4 Do you agree that teen-age consumers are a "follow-the-leader" group? Why or why not?

5 Based upon your reading, defend or criticize the statement: "Advertising is, to a great extent, responsible for the high level of production and consumption in the United States, but controls, both within and without the advertising industry, are necessary to protect the consumer."

CHAPTER 3

HOW ARE PRICES
DETERMINED?

Classical economic theory, describing a free market economy, contends that prices are determined solely by the laws of supply and demand. The economy of the United States, not conforming to classical economic principles, can best be described as a "mixed economy". This means that, while most segments of it are privately owned and operated, others are privately owned but regulated by government, and still others are owned by the government. In some of the privately owned manufacturing sectors, production is dominated by small numbers of large corporations. Thus, depending on the conditions under which goods and services are produced and sold, price determination within the American economic system varies widely from theoretically pure competition.

Public utility rates are determined by regulatory agencies and are set to cover costs plus a "reasonable" return. Furthermore, prices for wheat and cotton, likely to be very directly sensitive to changes in supply and demand, are supported by federal price support programs. The price of a share of stock sold on the New York Stock Exchange also responds directly to demand and supply pressures. Yet, specific safeguards are used to limit the range of fluctuations which occur on the New York Stock Exchange.

The competitive bidding that characterizes price determination on the commodity and stock exchanges can be misleading. Some students are likely to conclude that all prices are determined in the same manner. But many prices—e.g., window glass, bread, and milk—are rarely determined in a purely competitive manner.

The readings illustrate a continuum of opinions ranging between the extreme feeling of people who favor a free market and those who deny that a free market actually exists.

The first reading, by economist and columnist Henry Hazlitt, was published in February 1967. Here, he defends the free market theory by saying that over an appreciable time period, prices will automatically adjust themselves if supply and demand are allowed to operate freely.

The second selection is taken from material that economist Gardiner C. Means presented at a United States Senate hearing in 1957. Generally credited with the creation and popularization of the term "administered price", Means questions whether the prices of some products do, in fact, adjust to competitive forces, even over lengthy time periods.

In 1962, Means published *Pricing Power and the Public Interest,* in which he criticized the use of administered prices in the steel industry. The third selection, antagonistic to Means' thesis, is a review of his book by William H. Peterson, chief economist of the United States Steel Corporation.

The fourth reading, by Estes Kefauver, appeared in June 1958. Kefauver was chairman of the Senate Subcommittee on Antitrust and Monopoly that investigated price increases in the steel industry during the 1950's.

Although Means, Peterson, and Kefauver focus on the steel industry, other industries have been accused of administering prices to avoid competitive results. Almost all industries requiring a large investment in fixed capital—except public utilities—have been subjected to nearly the same accusation.

The final selection is by John Kenneth Galbraith, professor of economics at Harvard University and prominent author. This excerpt was taken from *The New Industrial State*, published in 1967. Galbraith describes what he believes are the primary factors in price determination in major industries of the United States.

**HOW SHOULD
PRICES BE DETERMINED?**

Abridged from "How Should Prices Be Determined?" by Henry Hazlitt from THE FREEMAN (February 1967). Reprinted by permission of The Foundation for Economic Education, Inc.

1 According to Hazlitt, how do high profits tend to reduce prices?
2 Would Hazlitt agree with the statement, "Monopoly price is usually higher than competitive price"? Why or why not?
3 According to Hazlitt, how do supply and demand determine price?

"How should prices be determined?" To this question we could make a short and simple answer: Prices should be determined by the market. . . .

Let us begin on the elementary level and say that prices are determined by supply and demand. If the relative demand for a product increases, consumers will be willing to pay more for it. Their competitive bids will both oblige them individually to pay more for it and enable producers to get more for it. This will raise the profit margins of the producers of that product. This, in turn, will tend to attract more firms into the manufacture of that product, and induce existing firms to invest more capital into making it.

The increased production will tend to reduce the price of the product again, and to reduce the profit margin in making it. The increased investment in new manufacturing equipment may lower the cost of production. Or—particularly if we are concerned with some extractive industry such as petroleum, gold, silver, or copper—the increased demand and output may raise the cost of production. In any case, the price will have a definite effect on demand, output, and cost of production just as these in turn will affect price. All four— demand, supply, cost, and price—are interrelated. A change in one will bring changes in the others. . . .

Because the desire and need for, and the supply and cost of, every individual commodity or service are constantly changing, prices and price relationships are constantly changing. They are changing yearly, monthly, weekly, daily, hourly. People who think that prices normally rest at some fixed point, or can be easily held to some "right" level, could profitably spend an hour watching the ticker tape of the stock market, or reading the daily report in the newspapers of what happened yesterday in the foreign exchange market, and in the markets for coffee, cocoa, sugar, wheat, corn, rice, and eggs. . . . They will find that none of these prices ever stands still. . . .

Let us begin by considering governmental efforts to keep prices up, or to raise them. Governments most frequently try to do this for commodities that constitute a principal item of export from their countries. Thus Japan once did it for silk and the British Empire for natural rubber; Brazil has done it and still periodically does it for coffee; and the United States has done it and still does it for cotton and wheat. The theory is that raising the price of these export commodities can only do good and no harm domestically because it will raise the incomes of domestic producers and do it almost wholly at the expense of the foreign consumers.

All of these schemes follow a typical course. It is soon discovered that the price of the commodity cannot be raised unless the supply is first reduced. This may lead in the beginning to the imposition of acreage restrictions. But the higher price gives an incentive to producers to increase their average yield per acre by planting the supported product only on their most productive acres, and by more intensive employment of fertilizers, irrigation, and labor. When the government discovers that this is happening, it turns to imposing absolute quantitative controls on each producer. This is usually based on each producer's previous production over a series of years. The result of this quota system is to keep out all new competition; to lock all existing producers into their previous relative position, and therefore to keep production costs high by removing the chief mechanisms and incentives for reducing such costs. The necessary readjustments are therefore prevented from taking place.

Meanwhile, however, market forces are still functioning in foreign countries. Foreigners object to paying the higher price. They cut down their purchases of the valorized [fixed price] commodity from the valorizing country, and search for other sources of supply. The higher price gives an incentive to other countries to start producing the valorized commodity. Thus, the British rubber scheme led Dutch producers to increase rubber production in Dutch dependencies. This not only lowered rubber prices, but caused the British to lose permanently their previous monopolistic position. In addition, the British scheme aroused resentment in the United States, the chief consumer, and stimulated the eventually successful development of synthetic rubber. In the same way, without going into detail, Brazil's coffee schemes and America's cotton schemes gave both a political and a price incentive to other countries to initiate or increase production of coffee and cotton, and both Brazil and the United States lost their previous monopolistic positions. . . .

Now let us turn to governmental efforts to *lower* prices or at least to keep them from rising. These efforts occur repeatedly in most nations, not only in wartime, but in any time of inflation. The typical process is something like this. The government, for whatever reason, follows policies that increase the quantity of money and credit. This inevitably starts pushing up prices. But this is not popular with consumers. Therefore, the government promises that it will "hold the line" against further price increases. . . .

If a government continues to create more currency on the one hand while rigidly holding down prices with the other, it will do immense harm. And let us note also that even if the government is not inflating the currency, but tries to hold either absolute or relative prices just where they were, or has instituted an "incomes policy" or "wage policy" drafted in accordance with some mechan-

ical formula, it will do increasingly serious harm. For in a free market, even when the so-called price "level" is not changing, all prices
are constantly changing in relation to each other. They are respond-
ing to changes in costs of production, of supply, and of demand for
each commodity or service.

And these price changes, both absolute and relative, are
in the overwhelming main both necessary and desirable. For they
are drawing capital, labor, and other resources out of the production
of goods and services that are less wanted and into the production
of goods and services that are more wanted. They are adjusting the
balance of production to the unceasing changes in demand. They
are producing thousands of goods and services in the relative
amounts in which they are socially wanted. These relative amounts
are changing every day. Therefore the market adjustments and price
and wage incentives that lead to these adjustments must be changing every day. . . .

What governments never realize is that, so far as any individual commodity is concerned, the cure for high prices is high
prices. High prices lead to economy in consumption and stimulate
and increase production. Both of these results increase supply and
tend to bring prices down again.

Very well, someone may say; so government price control
in many cases is harmful. But so far you have been talking as if
the market were governed by perfect competition. But what of
monopolistic markets? What of markets in which prices are controlled or fixed by huge corporations? Must not the government
intervene here if only to enforce competition or to bring about the
price that real competition would bring if it existed?

The fears of most economists concerning the evils of "monopoly" have been unwarranted and certainly excessive. In the
first place, it is very difficult to frame a satisfactory definition of
economic monopoly. If there is only a single drug store, barber shop,
or grocery in a small isolated town (and this is a typical situation),
this store may be said to be enjoying a monopoly in that town. . . .

On the other hand, nearly all economic monopolies are limited by the possibility of substitution. If copper piping is priced too
high, consumers can substitute steel or plastic; if beef is too high,
consumers can substitute lamb; if the original girl of your dreams

rejects you, you can always marry somebody else. Thus nearly every person, producer, or seller may enjoy a quasi monopoly within certain inner limits, but very few sellers are able to exploit that monopoly beyond certain outer limits. . . . In real life competition is never perfect, but neither is monopoly. . . .

The real problem is not whether or not there is "monopoly" in the market, but whether there is monopolistic pricing. . . .

The theory that there can be such a thing as a monopoly price, higher than a competitive price would have been, is certainly valid. The real question is, how *useful* is this theory either to the supposed monopolist in deciding his price policies or to the legislator, prosecutor, or court in framing antimonopoly policies? The monopolist, to be able to exploit his position, must know what the "demand curve" *is* for his product. He does not know; he can only guess; he must try to find out by trial and error. And it is not merely the unemotional price response of the consumers that the monopolist must keep in mind; it is what the effect of his pricing policies will probably be in gaining the goodwill or arousing the resentment of the consumer. More importantly, the monopolist must consider the effect of his pricing policies in either encouraging or discouraging the entrance of competitors into the field. He may actually decide that his wisest policy in the long run would be to fix a price no higher than he thinks pure competition would set, and perhaps even a little lower.

In any case, in the absence of competition, no one *knows* what the "competitive" price would be if it existed. Therefore, no one knows exactly how much higher an existing "monopoly" price is than a "competitive" price would be, and no one can be sure whether it is higher at all! . . .

As to antimonopoly policy, whatever the present condition may be in other countries, I can testify that in the United States this policy shows hardly a trace of consistency. It is uncertain, discriminatory, retroactive, capricious, and shot through with contradictions. No company today, even a moderate sized company, can know when it will be held to have violated the antitrust laws, or why. It all depends on the economic bias of a particular court or judge.

There is immense hypocrisy about the subject. Politicians

make eloquent speeches against "monopoly." Then they will impose tariffs and import quotas intended to protect monopoly and keep out competition; they will grant monopolistic franchises to bus companies or telephone companies; they will approve monopolistic patents and copyrights; they will try to control agricultural production to permit monopolistic farm prices. Above all, they will not only permit but impose labor monopolies on employers, and legally compel employers to "bargain" with these monopolies; and they will even allow these monopolies to impose their conditions by physical intimidation and coercion. . . .

. . . "The end of the law," as John Locke reminded us in the seventeenth century, "is not to abolish or restrain, but to preserve and enlarge freedom." And so we can say today that in the economic realm, the aim of the law should not be to constrict, but to maximize price freedom and market freedom.

THE CONCEPT OF "ADMINISTERED PRICE"

Abridged from "The Concept of 'Administered Price'" -Gardiner C. Means. Hearings Before the Subcommittee on Anti-Trust and Monopoly of the Committee on the Judiciary —U.S. Senate, 85th Congress, lst Session, from ADMINISTERED PRICES (Part I), 1957.

1 Does Means believe that all prices are administered?
2 What conditions does he cite as tending to produce administered prices?
3 Does Means consider administered prices a benefit or an evil?

[An] "administered price" is a price set by someone, usually a producer or seller, and kept constant for a period of time and for a series of transactions. The opposite of an administered price is a market price, a price that fluctuates on the basis of supply and demand as these forces are felt in the market.

The prices of wheat or cotton in the central markets are market and not administered prices. They constantly adjust to equate supply and demand. It is a coincidence if a series of transactions take place at identical prices.

In contrast, an administered price is set, and may be kept constant for weeks or months at a time. Most of the prices you come in contact with every day are administered prices—the prices in the Senate restaurant, at your barbershop, and in your local stores. The prices of steel and automobiles at wholesale. In fact, most industrial prices are administered prices and so are a large portion of retail prices. Most wage rates would also be classed as a type of administered price. It is only in agriculture and some raw materials that the flexible market price is the usual type. . . .

Administered prices represent a way of doing business that leads to greater efficiency and higher standards of living. We could not have our big efficient department stores and mail-order houses if prices were not administered. . . . Administered prices are an essential part of our modern economy. The point . . . is . . . that we do not now know enough about how administered prices actually operate to be able to make good national policy in such economic fields as inflation, full employment, and enforcement of competition. . . .

Now administered prices are not new. Even in Adam Smith's day administered prices were known, but at that time they appear to have been a minor factor in the largely agricultural economy and were never taken into account in classical economic theory. . . . Today, the administered price is the most typical form of price and there is need to take this form into account both in economic theory and in economic policy. . . .

. . . Market forces will limit the range within which an administered price is likely to be set but they do not determine the price. Within a range, often quite large, the price maker can set his price higher or lower and within that range there is nothing in supply or demand . . . which decree[s] one price rather than another. . . .

. . . Once a company is in a position to administer prices, if it aims to maximize its profits, it may have to choose between higher immediate profits and higher profits over a longer period. And often it will forego immediate profits for future profits. This may well be what happened immediately after the recent war when the established automobile companies were faced with a demand for cars far in excess of what they could supply. Instead of raising their prices to the level that would have maximized their current profits, they kept prices well below what the traffic would bear.

Clearly these companies were not required by market force to keep their prices so low. . . .

. . . Whenever a company is large enough in relation to its market to be vulnerable to governmental action under our anti-trust laws, it may well choose to set prices lower than the most profitable for fear of stimulating Government intervention. This can further widen the discrepancy between the classical price and the actual price set . . . .

. . . Some people have argued that inflation is solely a matter of the money supply and fiscal policy—that if the public's buying power in the form of liquid assets is increased, prices will rise; if buying power is reduced, prices will fall; and if the right amount of liquid assets is maintained prices will be stable.

This is good classical doctrine and if prices were actually controlled by market forces—if there were not a significant area of pricing discretion—I would be inclined to accept it.

But with the discretion implicit in administered prices, it would be possible to have a rise of prices without a prior increase in the public demand for goods. We have already seen that, by keeping their prices on the low side of the area of discretion, business can retard an inflation arising from too much buying power, as happened in the case of administered prices immediately after the war. . . .

Classical theorists believed that market forces operated in such a way as to make the economic system self-correcting. If unemployment were excessive, reduced demand would lead to a general fall in prices and wage rates. This, in turn, would increase the real buying power of the money supply and stimulate real demand for goods and production at the lower level of prices.

Thus, excessive unemployment was regarded as only a temporary and self-correcting matter. So far as I can see, this view would be correct if prices were continuously determined by market forces as the classical theorists assumed. . . .

. . . [Administered] prices lie quite outside the realm of traditional economic thinking and present serious problems which cannot find solution within the realm of traditional theory. There is need to find out more about this type of behavior. Why are administered prices changed when they are changed? Why not sooner? Why not later? And by what amounts are they changed and why not more or why not less? What are the factors which enter into these decisions and what is the latitude of discretion on the part of the price administrator?

**STEEL PRICE
ADMINISTRATION:
MYTH AND REALITY**

Abridged from "Steel Price Administration: Myth and Reality" by William H. Peterson, from MODERN AGE (Spring 1963). Reprinted by permission of Modern Age.

1 What is Peterson's attitude toward government and administered prices?
2 What is *non-price* competition?
3 In his summary, Peterson states that "(a) the concept of administered price is not sustained by the evidence" and "(d) administered prices have long been part of the American industrial economy. . . ." Are those statements contradictory? Explain.

Gardiner C. Means' *Pricing Power and the Public Interest* is Louis D. Brandeis' "curse of bigness" of a half-century ago all over again. The major Means' premise, in a nutshell, is the breakdown of effective competition in big business. His thesis is: bigness equals administered prices, administered prices equals administrative inflation, and administrative inflation necessitates a restructuring of U.S. manufacturing, beginning with the steel industry. . . .

Notwithstanding the weight of academic and business opinion arrayed against the doctrine of administered prices, the administration and certain influential members of Congress have not taken kindly to industrial price administrators, especially in the steel industry.

Perhaps the first irony to be noted in this development is that the government itself is a price administrator par excellance, but there is not a scintilla of criticism in the Means' book on this score. Yet the government administers utility and natural gas prices, and taxi, railroad, bus, and airline fares. It administers tax schedules, postal rates, and the salary schedules of civil servants. It administers the prices of publications issued by the U.S. Government Printing

Office. . . . The government's tariffs, import quotas, farm policy, and stockpiling programs also appear to be aimed at administering or propping prices in one way or another. . . .

Thus, government policy on prices is, broadly, to keep them up. In wartime, of course, it is to keep prices down. Another basic Means' contention lies in his view that competition in big business is anemic, that it is competition among the few, that the very existence of administered prices is proof that competition is ineffectual, which must be news to industrial executives. . . .

Consider the application of the administered price concept to Dr. Means' selected industry—steel. What concerns Dr. Means is that the price of steel is seemingly unresponsive to shifts in demand, for when the operating capacity falls because of lower demand—say, from 75 to 50 per cent of rated capacity—Dr. Means assumes that prices should also fall in accordance with the theory that a lower demand would lead to lower prices. To an extent, and quite an extent, steel prices do fall in the form of price shadings, discounts, additional services, freight absorption, and the like, and when demand is vigorous these various shadings disappear. But Dr. Means is quite correct in his observation that prices do not fluctuate very much in the short run, as does, say, the price of wheat at the Chicago Board of Trade. The result, says Dr. Means, is neither competition nor monopoly; it is "administrative competition." . . .

And is competition a function of corporate size and numbers? In terms of numbers, the American automotive industry has decreased from hundreds of producers to five. . . . But it is inaccurate to assume, as Dr. Means implicitly does, that there are but five automotive producers competing for sales in the United States, or that there are but a dozen large steel producers competing in the U.S. market. For, especially in the last few years, it has been evident that General Motors and other American auto producers must compete against Volkswagen, Fiat, Renault, and some forty other foreign car producers, and U.S. Steel and the other American steel producers must contend with the Steel Company of Wales, Phoenix-Rheinrohr of West Germany, Fuji Iron and Steel of Japan, as well as many other foreign steel producers. . . .

Yet, Dr. Means persists in referring to competition in the

American steel industry as gray, as administrative competition, as competition marked by difficulty of entry. True, entry is difficult, but not impossible. U.S. Steel's share of the market in the six decades of its existence had slipped from 60 per cent in 1901 to less than 30 per cent in 1961. Today there are more than 275 individual steel companies with plants located in 300 communities in 35 states engaged in the production and finishing of steel. . . .

Not only does Dr. Means minimize the substantial price competition which exists in the steel industry, but he also overlooks the importance of non-price competition. . . . Quality competition . . . is an important element of modern competition, frequently providing more value at a uniform market price. Greater value can also spring from more service provided by a seller—swifter delivery perhaps, tighter guarantees, better servicing, etc. . . .

. . . [Competition] from other materials has forged ahead. Aluminum cans are now in wide use for frozen citrus fruit concentrates, motor oils, and beer. Also competing against steel are plastics —from bottle caps to complete bottles. One-way glass bottles for beer and soft drinks are also competing for the can market. . . . Prestressed concrete has made gains in construction, again at the expense of steel. Aluminum, too, as a structural element has made its appearance in bridges. . . .

This brief review of competitive moves by and against steel producers does not seem to bear out the weak "administrative competition" Dr. Means finds in the steel industry. Perhaps the Means' definition of an industry is too narrow. Indeed, in the final analysis, perhaps an industry ought to be defined as "who competes with whom?" Thus . . . steel, aluminum, paperboard, prestressed concrete, fiberglass, plastics, etc., could be lumped into the structural materials industry. Each one of these materials has had a powerful competitive impact on steel, causing structural shifts in steel demand . . . .

In sum, this supplementary critique of administered prices concludes that (a) the concept of administered prices is not sustained by the evidence, (b) "administrative competition" is far more vigorous than Dr. Means assumes, (c) the real price administrator in our economy is not nearly so much the United States Steel Corporation or other big businesses as it is the United States Government, and (d) administered prices have long been part of the American industrial economy in particular and capitalistic economies in general.

A SENATOR DESCRIBES THE CONSEQUENCES OF A "MANIPULATED PRICE RISE"

"The Manipulated Price Rise" by Estes Kefauver, from THE NATION (June 28, 1958). Reprinted by permission of The Nation.

1 What is Kefauver's chief criticism of administered prices?
2 How does Kefauver attempt to disprove the contention that market price is determined by supply and demand?
3 How does Roger Blough define a competitive price?

Steel is an example of an "administered price" . . . .

It should be emphasized that administered prices are not undesirable *per se*. . . . But what concerns some of us in the Senate is *how* they are administered.

In the steel industry, at least, they have for many years been administered in only one direction—upward. . . . [Since] 1947 the price of steel has risen from year to year at almost a constant rate. It rose while unit labor costs were declining, and it rose while demand was falling. . . .

In too many industries throughout the country—steel, automobiles, oil, to name but a few— . . . price increases are made in the face of falling demand and substantial excess capacity. . . .

In our examination into the 1957 price increase, the subcommittee found that the increase in price was substantially in excess of the increase in labor costs resulting from the rise in wages and other benefits as provided for in the second year of the three-year contract between the steel companies and the United Steelworkers of America. . . .

In a presumably competitive industry, the question obviously arises as to how prices can in fact rise when demand is falling. If the price is raised, is it not reasonable to presume that there will be at least one substantial producer who will not go along with the increase? He would reap the benefit of his moderation by taking customers away from his competitors, thereby increasing his sales, reducing his overhead costs and swelling his profits. But this is not in fact what occurred in the steel industry, the oil industry, the automobile industry, or in any other industry examined by our subcommittee.

In all these various fields, the price leader sets the pace and the other producers follow more or less in lockstep. In our investigations, we found that the price increases by the other steel firms in the summer of 1957 were identical in nearly every instance with those established by the U.S. Steel Corp. Not a single instance was found in which a major producer ended up with a lower price for any steel product than the U.S. Steel price.

This parallelism of behavior was rationalized by the steel companies on the grounds that they were simply "meeting competition." This is an argument which has some force when the direction of the price change is downward. Obviously, if U.S. Steel reduced its price, the other steel companies must do likewise or lose business. But a number of Senators, including myself, were hard put to it to understand how the same line of reasoning could apply when the direction of change was upward. We could not quite understand why it was necessary for the other steel producers to raise their prices by the same amount and to the exact same level as U.S. Steel in order to be "competitive." We expressed the thought that they would be more competitive if they raised their price slightly *less* than U.S. Steel. . . .

Our difficulty in understanding this rationalization was intensified by the admission on the part of the steel companies that different steel firms had different costs. We could not understand why Bethlehem and National, which had higher profit rates than U.S. Steel and were apparently somewhat more efficient in their operations, found it necessary to raise their prices by the same amount as U.S. Steel. Moreover, Bethlehem and National are the nation's largest producers of certain particular steel products. On these products we could not understand why they permitted U.S. Steel, a lesser producer, to act as the price leader.

Fundamentally, our inability to understand these questions must be attributed to our difficulty in understanding the steel industry's concept of competition. This concept was nowhere more clearly set forth than by Roger Blough, Chairman of the Board of U.S. Steel, when he explained that "a price that matches another price is a competitive price."

MARKET PLANNING AND THE ROLE OF GOVERNMENT

Abridged from "Market Planning and the Role of Government" by John Kenneth Galbraith from THE NEW INDUSTRIAL STATE. Reprinted by permission of the publisher, Houghton Mifflin Company.

1 According to Galbraith, how are prices determined?
2 Does he support or oppose administered prices?
3 Why does Galbraith contend that when prices for a product are set by a few large firms there is a danger of uncontrolled price increases?

The principal planning instrument in the modern economy is the large corporation. Within broad limits, it determines what the consumer shall have and at what price he shall have it. And it foresees the need for and arranges the necessary supply of capital, machinery, and materials. . . .

Let us consider first the regulation of prices in the modern economy and the means by which public behavior is accommodated to plan. . . .

The power to set minimum industrial prices exists whenever a small number of firms share a market. The innocent at the universities have long been taught that small numbers of firms in the market—oligopoly, as it is known—accord to sellers the same power in imperfect form that has anciently been associated with monopoly. The principal difference is the imperfect nature of this monopoly power. It does not permit the exploitation of the consumer in quite such efficient fashion as was possible under the patents of monopoly accorded by the first Elizabeth to her favorites or by John D. Rockefeller to himself. . . .

. . . Professor Paul Samuelson, the most distinguished of contemporary economists, warns in his famous textbook on economics that "to reduce the imperfections of competition" (by which he means markets consisting of a small number of large firms or oligopoly) "a nation must struggle perpetually and must ever maintain vigilance." Since American markets are now dominated by a very small number of very large firms, the struggle, obviously, has been a losing one and is now lost. But the result is that the economy functions very well. . . .

. . . Prices in the modern economy are controlled not for the purposes of monopolistic exploitation. They are controlled for purposes of planning. . . . Modern industrial planning both requires and rewards great size. This means, in turn, that a comparatively small number of large firms will divide the production of most (though not all) products. Each, as a matter of ordinary prudence, will act with full consideration of its own needs and of the common need. Each must have control of its own prices. Each will recognize this to be a requirement of others. Each will foreswear any action, and notably any . . . competitive price-cutting, which would be prejudicial to the common interest in price control. This control is not difficult either to achieve or to maintain. Additionally, one firm's prices are another firm's costs. So, stability in prices means stability in costs.

The fact of control is far more important than the precise level at which prices are established. In 1964 in the United States, the big automobile companies had profits on their sales ranging from 5 percent to over 10 percent. There was security against collapse of prices and earnings for firms at either level. Planning was possible at either level of return. All firms could function satisfactorily. But none could have functioned had the price of a standard model fluctuated, depending on whim and reaction to the current novelties, from, say, $1800 to $3600, with steel, glass, chrome, plastics, paint, tires, stereo music, and labor moving over a similar range.

However, the level of prices is not unimportant. And from time to time, in response to major changes in cost—often when the renegotiation of a wage contract provides a common signal to all firms in the industry—prices must be changed. The prices so established will reflect generally the goals of those who guide the enterprise, not of the owners but of those who make the decisions. Security of earnings will be a prime objective. . . . The next most important goal will be the growth of the firm. This is almost certainly more important than maximum profits. The professional managers and technicians who direct and guide the modern firm do not themselves get the profits. These accrue mainly to the shareholders. But the managers and technicians do get the benefits of expansion. This brings the prestige which is associated with a larger firm and which is associated with growth as such. And as a very practical matter, it opens up new executive jobs, new opportunities for promotion, and better excuses for higher pay.

Prices, accordingly, will be set with a view to attracting customers and expanding sales. . . . Planning calls for stability of prices and costs, security of return, and expansion. With none of these is the consumer at odds. . . .

I must mention here one practical consequence of this argument, namely, its bearing on legal action against monopoly. There is a remarkable discrimination in the way such measures, notably the antitrust laws, are now applied. A great corporation wielding vast power over its markets is substantially immune. It does not appear to misuse its power; accordingly, it is left alone. And in any case, to declare all large corporations illegal is, in effect, to declare the modern economy illegal. That is rather impractical—and would damage any President's consensus. But if two small firms making the same product seek to unite, this corporate union will be meticulously scrutinized. And very possibly, it will be forbidden. This may be so even though the merged firm is miniscule in size or market power as compared with the giant that is already a giant.

The explanation is that the modern antimonopoly and antitrust laws are substantially a charade. Their function is not to prevent exploitation of the public. If great size and great market power led to such exploitation, our case would long since have been hopeless. Their function is to persuade people, liberal economists in particular, that the market still exists, for here is the state vigilantly standing guard. It does so by exempting the large firms and swatting those that seek to become larger.

The French, Germans, and Japanese either do not have or do not enforce such laws. That is because they are not impelled similarly to worship at the altar of the market. They quietly accept the logic of planning and its requirements in size for effective market control. There is no indication that they suffer in consequence.

62

When prices for a particular product are set by a few large firms, there is little danger of price-cutting. This part of the control is secure. There does remain a danger of uncontrolled price increases.

In particular, when a few large firms bargain with a strong union, conflict can be avoided by acceding to union demands. And there is not much incentive to resist. There is a common understanding among the firms that all will raise their prices to compensate for such a settlement. If demand is strong enough to keep the economy near full employment, it will be strong enough to make such price increases feasible. These price increases, in turn, set in motion demands for further wage increases. Thus, the familiar upward spiral of wages and prices proceeds. And this too is prejudicial to planning. The individual firm, moreover, cannot prevent such price increases; they are beyond its control as a planning unit.

So here, more and more we follow the practice of the formally planned economies. We rely on the state to set maximum wages and prices. . . . Economists accord it little or no standing in economic policy. They say it interferes with the market. Unions also dislike it: they say it interferes with free collective bargaining. Businessmen disapprove: they say it interferes with their natural freedom of decision on prices. But what everyone opposes in principle, all advanced countries end up doing in practice. The answer once more is clear. In a market economy, such ceilings would be unnecessary. But they are an indispensable counterpart of economic planning and of the minimum price control that already exists.

QUESTIONS FOR CLOSER STUDY

1 Does Kefauver's evidence support or oppose Galbraith's theory of price determination?

2 Which explanation of prices seems least realistic? Why?

3 "All of the articles contain some truth, but no single article can be considered a complete explanation." Explain why you agree or disagree with the statement.

4 For each of the following select the theory (or parts of theories) contained in the readings that best explain(s) its price in today's consumer market: (a) gasoline, (b) color TV set, (c) transistor radio, (d) 7-room ranch house in suburban Chicago, (e) electricity

rates, (f) airplane fare from New York to Rome, Italy, (g) nylon rug, (h) house paint, (i) light bulb, (j) automobile tire, (k) men's shoes, (l) refrigerator. (Note: In some cases it may be argued that no theory is influential.)

5 "With automobiles non-price competition has benefited the consumer." Indicate why you agree or disagree.

CHAPTER 4

HOW CAN WE
RESCUE OUR CITIES?

Although the United States has always had a mobile population, a dramatic increase in the movement of people has occurred since World War II. Millions of middle-class white families have moved from large cities to suburbs; and their exodus has been paralleled by an influx of low-income, largely rural families, both white and non-white. As a result, the composition of most large cities has changed drastically. Two of the most alarming consequences of this change are declining municipal operating funds and growing social and economic needs.

Schools are badly in need of repair or replacement. Inadequate street repairs, air pollution, sewage disposal, and substandard housing are equally critical problems that confront officials in every major city. The ability of the cities to cope with these problems is seriously impaired by fragmented and ineffective local government structures. Gradually losing the financial support of great numbers of the relatively affluent middle class and taking on the burdens of economically deprived residents, the cities are not strong enough to initiate or finance programs. Recent riots indicate the depth of the problem.

WHAT KIND OF CITIES DO WE WANT?

TESTIMONY ON THE "DEMONSTRATION CITIES" BILL

WE'D RATHER DO IT OURSELVES

URBAN UNREST: WHOSE PROBLEM IS IT?

WHAT CAN BE DONE?

There is general agreement that we can and must rescue our cities, but there is also widespread disagreement over both responsibility for and control of municipal problems. Responsibility implies a sensitivity to the problem—that is, an ability to respond realistically to the needs of the people. Control implies an ability to assume financial control of the problems that loom so large. Most cities are relatively poor, and their ability to meet the financial demands of their people is weak; however, because city officials are close to the problem, they are most likely of all public office holders to know what needs to be done. In comparison, the federal treasury is rich, but its administrators are far away from the people who need the funds.

The problems inherent in assuming responsibility are essentially political: what forms should government take to be most responsible to the people's needs? The problems inherent in assuming control are essentially economic: how does government assume and maintain financial control of urban problems? Saving our cities is clearly not a problem that can be answered with either responsibility or control; it must be met with certain elements of each. Nevertheless, we cannot consider all aspects of the problem in this chapter. The following readings are concerned, primarily, with the matter of control: who is best able to pay for the kind of social and economic growth that our cities need?

The first reading, part of a report published in the April 1967 issue of *Nation's Cities,* is critical of some current municipal practices and suggests some solutions to the problem.

The second reading was taken from a statement made in February 1967 by Robert C. Weaver who, as Secretary of Housing and Urban Development, testified at a meeting of the Subcommittee on Housing of the House Committee on Banking and Currency. Supporting the demonstration cities bill, which subsequently became law, Weaver strongly advocated federal financing of urban renewal.

The third selection appeared in the September 1965 issue of *Nation's Business*. Opposing the extension of federal influence, it supports local financing of urban development.

The fourth reading is excerpted from a speech by L. W. Moore, president of the American Oil Company. Addressing the 1967 Institute for Management at Northwestern University, he urged businessmen to assume responsibility on the local level and to support local programs financially.

The last article is from the 1968 Report of the National Advisory Commission on Civil Disorders, which is also known as the Kerner Report. It outlines the difficulties facing local governments and recognizes that cooperation of other sectors of the community and the state is necessary in solving urban problems.

 WHAT KIND OF CITIES DO WE WANT?

Abridged from "What Kind of Cities Do We Want?" from NATION'S CITIES (April 1967). Reprinted by permission of Nation's Cities.

1 Why is the property tax a major problem in many American cities?
2 Do you agree with the writer's definition of a "local problem"? Why or why not?
3 Explain why you agree or disagree with the concluding sentence: "We could get much better cities much sooner if our cities would just stop subsidizing their worst faults."

A more chaotic chaos would be hard to dream up than the chaos over what government should do what, and what government should pay for what, to meet our urban needs.

Responsibility is divided horizontally four ways between

local, county, state and federal government. It is divided verti-
cally scores and sometimes hundreds of ways, first between the
central city government and all the surrounding town and village
governments, and then again between all these governments and a
still greater proliferation of special tax districts, administrations
and authorities—bridge authorities, park authorities, water districts, sewer districts, fire districts, school districts, library districts,
garbage districts, hospital districts, etc. Within the local governments, authority is often divided still further, with the school
board going its own way to spend more money than anyone else.
In Washington the same confusion is repeated. Both the Senate
and the House scatter responsibility for urban affairs legislation
among half a dozen uncoordinated committees. . . .

No city government collects anywhere near enough money
of its own to take on the whole job of coping with all problems that
confront it. One reason no city government has enough money is
that few states let the cities collect enough taxes, even if they want
to. The second reason is that few cities like to collect any more taxes
than they have to; they would rather get grants-in-aid from the
states or from Washington. The third reason is that most cities are
afraid to raise taxes for fear of speeding the exodus of industry.
The fourth reason is that the cities' only exclusive revenue source
is the property tax, and most states make their cities collect most of
their property taxes, not on land (which is undertaxed) but on improvements (which are already so overtaxed that the tax inhibits
even some of the most needed improvements). The fifth (and perhaps the biggest) reason is that in this country, local government
is stuck with enormous costs that in other countries are paid as a
matter of course by the central government, so, paradoxically, the
local tax burden in most cities is too high even though the tax take
is too low!

One result of keeping city governments poor is that too few
city services are good enough. A second is that few suburbs want
to be annexed to cities that can't afford good schools and other
top-grade services. The third result is the proliferation of special
tax districts to pay for services the cities have no money to provide
(Los Angeles has 246 of them). Fourth, cities are afraid to raise more
taxes even if they could, for fear of driving still more people and

businesses to tax havens in the suburbs. Fifth, many industries are moving to suburban tax havens anyhow. Finally, the sixth result is that nobody can tell just who is responsible for what. Schools, for example, are paid for partly by the local school district, partly by the state, a little by Washington, with the state setting the standards, the local authorities picking the teachers and the federal government decreeing the racial balance. . . .

One big reason so many city governments are too poor to pay their full part in making their cities pleasant for people and profitable for business is that, in the U S, most of the cost of public education is charged to local government . . . . These costs were small enough for local government to carry when few children went beyond eighth grade, and schooling meant mostly the three Rs; they are now far too heavy to charge against the revenues traditionally reserved for local government (i.e., the property tax), and they will soon redouble.

The United States is almost the only country on earth where the central government does not pay all the costs of free public education. . . .

A second reason why our city governments are too poor to make their local services good is that the local property tax is still being tapped for many of the costs of poverty and many of the costs required by today's much-more-generous spending for poor relief. . . .

Poverty and education are not local problems or local responsibilities in the same sense, or to anything like the same degree, that police and fire protection, water supply, garbage collection, . . . and urban mass transportation are local problems and local responsibilities. Half the people on relief in almost every city and half the ward patients in the city hospitals came there from somewhere else; half the children in the city schools came from somewhere else and will grow up to work somewhere else. . . .

If these not-primarily-local poverty and education costs were all paid by the state and federal governments that call the tune for them, our local governments would have plenty of money of their own to cover all their own, strictly local costs and make all their own local services good without sending their mayors to the state capital or to Washington, hat in hand, to beg for subsidies. . . .

Living close requires more, rather than less, willingness to cooperate, to share the cost instead of trying to get away with something for nothing at somebody else's expense (usually the tax-payer's). The implications are enormous. For instance:

Industries, utilities and apartments should not expect to hold down their own costs by pouring tons of soot and garbage ash into the air to fall on somebody else's property, for someone else to pay for cleaning up. (In New York, this cleaning bill is officially estimated at $500 million a year; almost as much *each year* as it would cost to put smoke control devices on all the city's garbage incinerators and factory and utility chimneys.)

Towns and factories should not expect to save money by pouring untreated sewage and waste into our streams for someone else to purify for eventual reuse elsewhere downstream.

Drivers should not expect to foul up traffic by parking free or cheaply at other taxpayers' expense, on land priced up to $100 a square foot. As long as motorists can park free, or almost free, on busy streets, how can we expect them to pay by the hour for off-street parking? . . .

Transit riders should not expect to ride long distances for a fraction of the cost, by getting the city to subsidize most of the fare. (But all of us recognize that as long as commuting to the cities by expressway gets a subsidy running as high as 10 cents a car-mile, mass transportation will also have to be subsidized. It is much cheaper to subsidize mass transportation than to subsidize driving to work at the present scale.)

Most notoriously, upper-income commuters should not expect the state or federal government to subsidize their flight to the suburbs by paying half the cost of their commutation.

Urban landowners should not be allowed to get rich by getting other taxpayers to pay the cost of all the public facilities without which their land would be good only for market gardening, and not much good at that.

We all sympathize with the cities' money problems; we all agree that the cities need money relief from state and federal governments.

But too many of our cities' money problems are of their own making. Cities would need less money help from above if they could screw up their courage to stop subsidizing obsolescence, blight and sprawl by undertaxing valuable underused land, and subsidizing water waste, traffic jams, air pollution and water pollution by far-below-cost user charges. We could get much better cities much sooner if our cities would just stop subsidizing their worst faults.

**TESTIMONY ON THE
"DEMONSTRATION CITIES"
BILL**

"Pro: The Question of the New Federal Program" by Robert C. Weaver. From *Congressional Digest*, Vol. 46, No. 2 (February 1968). "Controversy Over the New Federal Program for Demonstration Cities, Pro and Con."

1 In the bill that Weaver supports, what requirements were included to insure effective use of federal funds?
2 How did the bill attempt to meet the criticism that federal financing means federal control?
3 What does Weaver mean by his statement, "the cities with the greatest slum problems have the least capacity to deal with those problems"?

The demonstration cities bill is the most important proposal in the President's program to assist in rebuilding American cities. It has focused the interest of the Congress and the entire Nation on the most critical domestic problem facing the United States—the need to improve the quality of urban life. . . .

The demonstration cities bill would provide to the cities—

First, Federal funds to cover up to 90 per cent of the cost of planning and developing comprehensive city demonstration programs.

Second, special Federal grants, supplementing assistance available under existing grant-in-aid programs. . . .

Third, Federal grants to cover all the costs of providing relocation adjustment payments to those persons, families, and businesses displaced by activities which are a part of these programs.

Fourth, technical assistance to help carry out these programs.

A comprehensive city demonstration program is a locally prepared and scheduled program for rebuilding or restoring entire sections and neighborhoods of slum and blighted areas through the concentrated and coordinated use of all available Federal aids and local private and governmental resources. It will include citywide aids and resources necessary to improve the general welfare of the people living or working in these areas.

The assistance provided by this bill will help cities of all sizes to plan, develop, and carry out programs to rebuild or revitalize large slum or blighted areas and to expand and improve public programs and services available to the people who live in these areas. It will provide funds needed for the city to participate in existing Federal assistance programs. . . .

The comprehensive city demonstration programs carried out under this bill would provide massive additions to the supply of decent, low-, and moderate-cost housing. . . .

In order to qualify for assistance under this legislation, a city must be prepared to plan and carry out a comprehensive city demonstration program. This will be a local program; planned, and carried out by local people; and based on local judgment as to the city's needs and its order of priorities in meeting these needs. . . .

It will be necessary for a city to embark on major new undertakings addressed to major urban problems. This legislation is designed to help those cities willing to face up to their responsibilities—willing and able to bring together all the public and private bodies whose joint action is necessary to solve their problems—willing to fully commit their energy and resources—willing to undertake actions which will have widespread and profound effects on the social and physical structure of the city.

. . . In preparing their demonstration programs, cities will have to—

First, examine their substantive laws to determine the extent to which those laws impede substantial progress in carrying out their demonstration programs and to take appropriate action, if necessary, to make those laws consistent with the objectives of their programs. . . .

Second, apply high standards of design to buildings constructed and rehabilitated under the program in order to maintain distinctive natural, historical, and cultural characteristics. . . .

Third, make maximum use of new and improved technology and design, including the introduction of cost-reduction techniques to every aspect of a city's activities. . . .

Fourth, encourage good community relations and counteract the segregation of housing by race or income.

The physical rebuilding and restoration of our cities should be accompanied by appropriate actions to narrow the housing gap between the poor and disadvantaged and the rest of the community. Nondiscrimination in any housing assisted under a demonstration program is a legal requirement. . . .

Fifth, indicate that the projects and activities carried on under the program are consistent with comprehensive planning for the entire urban or metropolitan area. . . .

A comprehensive city demonstration program will not replace existing Federal programs which now assist cities to provide for their urban development and growth. Rather, it will supplement and tend to encourage the focusing and coordination of existing programs, such as the urban renewal, mass transit, antipoverty, and health and welfare programs, in rebuilding and revitalizing urban areas. . . .

The great problems confronting the Nation's cities are well known.

Slums and blight are widespread. Persons of low income concentrate increasingly in the older urban areas. Housing and community facilities and services are inadequate. . . .

At the same time as the need for city services grows, the city's ability to provide these services is impaired by the very blight that creates the demand. Greater blight—greater demand for city services—decreasing revenues to meet the demand—that is the downward trend in many American cities. In these circumstances, it is not surprising that the cities with the greatest slum problems have the least capacity to deal with those problems. . . .

The city plays a critical role in American life. It must provide jobs and adequate housing and education for millions of the Nation's unemployed, ill housed, and uneducated. It must provide community facilities and health and social services on a scale unprecedented in the Nation's history. And, it must do so in the face of overwhelming demands on its skills and resources.

The success of the city in providing the physical and social framework through which millions of poor and disadvantaged

Americans are prepared to participate fully in the Nation's life—is a vital national concern.

**WE'D RATHER
DO IT OURSELVES**

© 1965, Nation's Business—the Chamber of Commerce of the United States. Condensed from the September issue.

1 What reasons does Mayor Hasselberg give for refusing federal aid for Bloomington? Indicate whether you agree or disagree with his reasons.
2 What difficulties do cities encounter in undertaking self-help programs?
3 What was the role of voter education in these cities' decisions?

Editors of *Nation's Business* talked with mayors and other elected officials of eight . . . communities across the nation, with populations ranging as high as 200,000. . . .

In discussing their communities, the officials offered a broad range of reasons for their opposition to federal handouts. . . .

"A city that takes urban renewal money from Washington when it doesn't need it is no more ethical than a person who chisels on public relief."

That's the opinion of Donald R. Hasselberg, mayor of Bloomington, Minn., a city of 67,000 people near Minneapolis.

Mayor Hasselberg is a slide-rule-wielding corporate accountant whose background in accountancy has made him a diligent student of municipal finances—his own and others'.

Study of the federal government's own figures, he says, proves that many cities receiving urban renewal aid from Washington are perfectly capable of paying their own way and, in some cases, are free of any debt.

In fact, he argues, some cities now pulling in millions in urban renewal assistance couldn't demonstrate a real need for the money "if an objective needs test were applied."

Bloomington, though rapidly growing and potentially eligible for federal money, has no federal urban renewal projects and doesn't want any, according to its 49-year-old mayor. He proudly points to the 22 schools built in Bloomington since 1950 and the fact that the city has met all of its local commitments through bond issues since that time. The city's physical layout embraces everything from farms to factories and industrial parks.

Mayor Hasselberg's review of urban renewal in other cities has convinced him that delays and red tape are more often the rule than the exception when a community decides to go the federal route. "More important," he continues, "is the appalling misconception on the part of many people that money they get from Washington is 'free.' They overlook the fact that Washington hasn't got any money that it didn't get from the people in the first place. And they overlook the fact that when this money is doled out to rich and poor communities alike a very inequitable financial base is laid. There are going to be some cities—a major Midwestern city comes to mind—that are going to get far more than they deserve."

With the attitude of "everybody's doing it" so widespread, why should any city, well-off or not, refrain from seeking federal dollars? Mayor Hasselberg answers his own question: "I believe those able to pay their own way have a moral responsibility not to go after Washington money just because it is there."

URBAN UNREST: WHOSE PROBLEM IS IT?

Abridged from "Urban Unrest: Whose Problem Is It?" By L. W. Moore, the commencement Address at Northwestern University School of Business (August 25, 1967). Reprinted by permission of L. W. Moore.

1 Is there a conflict between management's responsibility to its stockholders and its responsibilities to society? Why or why not?
2 Why does Moore consider productive employment a major goal in the struggle to rescue our cities?
3 How does the author think that the ultimate solution to the urban problem will be achieved?

I learned that you have devoted a great deal of time and thought this summer to discussions of the external environment in which business operates today. You have, so to speak, looked out of the world of business into the social universe that surrounds it.

Some of the things you have seen through this intellectual telescope have looked exceedingly grim. They have also raised some knotty questions. For example, and I might as well throw out a big one:

Does management, in the exercise of its responsibility to its stockholders, have the right to invest time, effort, and money to help solve broad social problems [i.e., urban problems]? . . .

I don't lose much sleep over this one, nor should any other executive if he will really think through what it's all about. For while we are in business to make a profit, and profit motivation is a tremendous social force, we cannot abdicate our responsibility to help create and maintain a continuing society that will enable us to operate profitably. We neglect our obligation to our stockholders if we take refuge in the cliche that our duty ends with today's production and sale of competitive commodities. . . .

But if, as David Rockefeller has suggested, "the business community has a critical stake in economic progress and an inescapable responsibility to contribute to it," what should the nature of that contribution be? . . .

At the outset, it should be said that I believe that the solution of the economic ills of a substantial segment of our population will be achieved only through the combined efforts of business and industry, government, social welfare organizations, churches, schools, and the responsible leadership in the Negro community itself. I also believe, however, that without the conscientious involvement of business and industry the activities that are undertaken are rather apt to be palliatives instead of cures.

This is not said critically, but simply because the only real long-term solution to the problem is employment; productive employment that will enable men who are now unskilled, unschooled, and unemployed to achieve a sense of dignity. . . .

Business must become involved because it is the ultimate source of these jobs, and the process of preparing the unskilled to assume them is one in which it must have a role. In the vernacular of the inner city streets, we're the cats with the bread, and because jobs are the answer we must help government, the schools, and the social agencies find ways to prepare people for the kind of work

76

that we will be able to provide. . . .

Business and industry also have knowledge, skills and technology that could be a powerful force in the solution of related urban problems—in housing, transportation and other areas that impinge on urban economic problems as a whole. . . . We should . . . help light more fires of hope in the inner city before the disillusioned Americans who live there touch off more costly fires of frustration and despair.

WHAT CAN BE DONE?

Abridged from the Report of the National Advisory Commission on Civil Disorders (Washington, D.C.: U.S. Government Printing Office, 1968).

1 Why did the Commission conclude that the problems of the cities cannot be solved solely by state and municipal governments?
2 How has "cost-cutting" increased, rather than decreased, the city's problems?
3 To what extent can it be said that the tax structure in most cities is a major problem?
4 Why are the city's service costs rising faster than factory production costs?

The racial disorders of last summer in part reflect the failure of all levels of government—federal and state as well as local—to come to grips with the problems of our cities. The ghetto symbolizes the dilemma: a widening gap between human needs and public resources and a growing cynicism regarding the commitment of community institutions and leadership to meet these needs.

The problem has many dimensions—financial, political and institutional. Almost all cities—and particularly the central cities of the largest metropolitan regions—are simply unable to meet the growing need for public services and facilities with traditional sources of municipal revenue. Many cities are structured politically so that great numbers of citizens—particularly minority groups—have little or no representation in the processes of government. Finally, many cities lack both the will and the capacity to use effectively the resources that are available to them.

Instrumentalities of federal and state government often compound the problems. National policy expressed through a very large number of grant programs and institutions rarely exhibits a coherent and consistent perspective when viewed at the local level. State efforts, traditionally focused on rural areas, often fail to tie in effectively with either local or federal programs in urban areas.

Meanwhile, the decay of the central city continues—its revenue base eroded by the retreat of industry and white middle-class families to the suburbs, its budget and tax rate inflated by rising costs and increasing numbers of dependent citizens and its public plant schools, hospitals and correctional institutions deteriorated by age and long deferred maintenance.

Yet to most citizens, the decay remains largely invisible. Only their tax bills and the headlines about crime or "riots" suggest that something may be seriously wrong in the city.

There are, however, two groups of people that live constantly with the problem of the city: the public officials and the poor, particularly the residents of the racial ghetto. Their relationship is a key factor in the development of conditions underlying civil disorders. . . .

. . . [Many] city governments are poorly organized to respond effectively to the needs of ghetto residents, even when these needs are made known to appropriate public officials. . . .

. . . [The] typical ghetto resident has complicated social and economic problems which often require the services of a whole variety of government and private agencies. At the same time, he may be unable to break down his problems in ways which fit the complicated structure of government. Moreover, he is often unaware of his rights and opportunities as they exist under public programs and unable to develop the necessary guidance from either public or private sources.

Current trends in municipal administration have had the effect of reducing the capacity of local government to respond effectively to these problems. The pressures for administrative efficiency and cost-cutting have brought about the withdrawal of many of the operations of city government from direct contact with neighborhood and citizen. The introduction of a merit system and a professionalized civil service has made the cities far more businesslike, but it has also tended to depersonalize government and isolate it from the individual. . . .

Local governments have had to bear a particularly heavy financial burden in the two decades since the end of World War II. All United States cities are highly dependent upon property taxes that are relatively unresponsive to changes in income. Consequently, growing municipalities have been hard-pressed for adequate revenues to meet rising demands for services generated by population increase. On the other hand, stable or declining cities have not only been faced with steady cost increases but also with a slow-growing, or even declining, tax base.

As a result of the population shifts of the post-war period, concentrating the more affluent parts of the urban population in residential suburbs while leaving the less affluent in the central cities, the increasing burden of municipal taxes frequently falls upon that part of the urban population least able to pay them.

Increasing concentrations of urban growth have called forth greater expenditures for every kind of public service: education, health, police protection, fire protection, parks, sewage disposal, sanitation, water supply, etc. These expenditures have strikingly outpaced tax revenues.

The story is summed up below:

Local Government Revenues, Expenditures and Debt
(Billions of dollars)

	1950	1966	Increase
Revenues	11.7	41.5	+29.8
Expenditures	17.0	60.7	+43.7
Debt outstanding	18.8	77.5	+58.7

The fact that the problems of the cities are a national problem is seen in the growth of federal assistance to urban areas under various grant-in-aid programs, which reached the level of $10 billion in the current fiscal year.

Nevertheless, the fiscal plight of many cities is likely to grow even more serious in the future. Local expenditures inevitably will continue to rise steeply as a result of several factors, including the difficulty of increasing productivity in the predominantly service activities of local governments, and the rapid technologically-induced increases in productivity in other economic sectors. . . .

In the postwar period, costs of the same units of output have increased very rapidly in certain key activities of local government. For example, education is the single biggest form of expenditure by local governments (including school districts), accounting for about 40 percent of their outlays. From 1947 to 1967, costs per pupil-day in United States public schools rose at a rate of 6.7 percent per year compounded—only slightly less than doubling every ten years. This major cost item is likely to keep on rising rapidly in the future, along with other government services like police, fire, and welfare activities.

Some increases in productivity may occur in these fields, and some economies may be achieved through use of semi-skilled assistants such as police and teachers' aides. Nevertheless, with the need to keep pace with private sector wage scales, local government costs will keep on rising sharply.

This and other future cost increases are important to future relations between central cities and suburbs. Rising costs will inevitably force central cities to demand more and more assistance from the federal government. But the federal government can obtain such funds through the income tax only from other parts of the economy. Suburban governments are experiencing the same cost increases along with the rising resentment of their constituents. . . .

For purposes of analysis, the Commission has defined three basic choices for the future . . . :

Under . . . the Present Policies Choice, the nation would maintain approximately the share of resources now being allocated to programs of assistance for the poor, unemployed and disadvantaged. . . .

Under . . . the Enrichment Choice, the nation would seek to offset the effects of continued Negro segregation and deprivation in large city ghettos. The Enrichment Choice would aim at creating dramatic improvements in the quality of life in disadvantaged central-city neighborhoods—both white and Negro. It would require marked increases in federal spending for education, housing, employment, job training, and social services. . . .

The Integration Choice—like the Enrichment Choice—would

call for large-scale improvement in the quality of ghetto life. But it would also involve both creating strong incentives for Negro movement out of central-city ghettos and enlarging freedom of choice concerning housing, employment, and schools. . . .

Any social and economic programs likely to have significant lasting effect would require very substantial annual appropriations for many years. Their cost would well exceed the direct losses sustained in recent civil disorders. Property damage in all the disorders we investigated, including Detroit and Newark, totalled less than $100 million. The casualty toll was far smaller than that for automobile accidents on an average weekend.

But it would be a tragic mistake to view the Present Policies Choice as cheap. Damage figures measure only a small part of the costs of civil disorder. They cannot measure the costs in terms of the lives lost, injuries suffered, minds and attitudes closed and frozen in prejudice, or the hidden costs of the profound disruption of entire cities.

Ultimately, moreover, the economic and social costs of the Present Policies Choice will far surpass the cost of the alternatives. The rising concentration of impoverished Negroes and other minorities within the urban ghettos will constantly expand public expenditures for welfare, law enforcement, unemployment and other existing programs without reversing the tendency of older city neighborhoods toward decay and the breeding of frustration and discontent. But the most significant item on the balance of accounts will remain largely invisible and incalculable—the toll in human values taken by continued poverty, segregation and inequality of opportunity. . . .

Finally, there remains the issue of leadership. Now, as never before, the American city has need for the personal qualities of strong democratic leadership. Given the difficulties and delays involved in administrative reorganization or institutional change, the best hope for the city in the short run lies in this powerful instrument. In most cities the mayor will have the prime responsibility. . . .

. . . As leader and mediator, he must involve all those groups —employers, news media, unions, financial institutions and others— which only together can bridge the chasm now separating the racial ghetto from the community. . . .

In this effort, state government has a vital role to play. It must equip city leadership with the jurisdictional tools to deal with its problems. It must provide a fuller measure of financial and other resources to urban areas. Most importantly, state leadership is in a unique position to focus the interests and growing resources, political as well as financial, of the suburbs on the physical, social, and cultural environment of the central cities. The crisis confronting city government today cannot be met without regional cooperation.

QUESTIONS FOR CLOSER STUDY

1 Is the federal government always better able to finance much-needed urban programs than are state and/or local governments?

2 Do cities the size and character of Bloomington reflect typical urban problems in the United States? Why or why not?

3 How do the conclusions reached by the President's Commission agree or disagree with recommendations made by L. W. Moore?

4 Should responsibility for and control of urban problems rest exclusively with one level of government or another? Why or why not?

5 What plan could you propose that would reconcile the different opinions expressed by Robert Weaver and by the selection from *Nation's Business?*

CHAPTER 5

HOW SHOULD
WE SLICE UP
THE ECONOMIC PIE?

The world's supply of resources is limited, yet man's wants seem to be unlimited. We are continually reminded of this basic economic problem as we read about labor's demands for better wages, management's concern for profits, stockholders' desire for greater dividends, and unemployed people's desperate need for a share of the economic pie. Practically every special interest group in our society feels that it is not getting a fair share of the nation's wealth.

Seventy-five years ago the division of the economic pie was a subject for debate only in very radical circles. A businessman would have confidently stated that it is not the business of government to participate in the division of wealth and that it is distributed according to the economic laws of nature. Individual wealth, he might have said, is the reward one receives for hard work, superior ability, and risk of capital. Poverty, he would have maintained, is the result of laziness, ignorance, or stupidity, and the poor will always be with us. If this view seems harsh, it was nevertheless as acceptable to the rugged individualist as Darwin's theory of the "survival of the fittest".

Many wealthy men felt strongly that it was their moral and religious responsibility to help those in need but that this was a matter of private conscience. To suggest that they be required to do so through some artificial device of wealth distribution would have been considered revolutionary and immoral.

Today, government has assumed greater responsibility for welfare and other allocation of funds, and this change has aroused a lively controversy. Some people think that government is not doing enough, either in welfare to the needy or in the solution of other urgent problems. Pointing out the existence of hunger, slums, and pollution—as well as other conditions inconsistent with American wealth—they claim that private industry has failed to live up to its responsibilities in helping eliminate these evils and that government must accept major responsibility in this area.

Others contend that government distribution of wealth is leading the country down the road to socialism and the welfare state. They argue that private industry is better able to raise the level of prosperity for all people than is the government. They point out that the American economy is the most powerful and affluent the world has ever known and that most of the people share in this prosperity.

The problem of the distribution of wealth is not, however, confined to a debate over the role of government. Labor wants higher wages; businessmen want to retain more profits; the consumer wants his share in the form of lower prices; the aged want greater financial security; and so on. The readings in this chapter present some of the arguments over the slicing of the economic pie.

The first reading, by Charles G. Mortimer, a director of the General Foods Corporation, was published in 1962. Mortimer maintains that profits, reinvested in industry, result in increased production and thus lower prices—which benefit all people.

The second selection, written by prominent economist and author Robert L. Heilbroner, first appeared in the August 29, 1964, issue of *Saturday Review*. In his article, Heilbroner suggests a new approach to the problems of wealth distribution.

The third article is an excerpt from John Kenneth Galbraith's 1958 book, *The Affluent Society*. Galbraith cites the inequities in American society and pleads for social balance.

The last reading, from an article by George J. Stigler, professor of economics at the University of Chicago, was published in 1966. Stigler presents the positions of the so-called "liberal" and "conservative" groups on the question of wealth distribution, and he claims that these groups are not engaged in a legitimate debate—but are merely propagandizing their own views.

THE INDISPENSABLE FUNCTION OF PROFITS

"The Indispensable Function of Profits" by Charles G. Mortimer from VITAL SPEECHES OF THE DAY (September 1962). Reprinted by permission of City News Publishing Co.

1 Does the author feel that conflict exists in the American economy?
2 In what ways does the average American share indirectly in the prosperity of business?
3 According to the author, what are the common goals of both business and labor?

We need to dispel the most harmful of all the myths that have been handed down from the past—the myth which holds that conflict *must* exist between economic groups under capitalism. This belief is founded on another century's concept of capitalism. It utterly ignores the simple fact that what we have in the United States today is what has been aptly called a People's Capitalism. Ours is a system in which the savings of millions of men and women in all walks of life provide the capital for investment in the various industries and businesses of America.

Like it or not, our profit system is on trial before the world today. To prove it is successful, we must shake our economy out of its current sluggishness. This will be a do-it-yourself job, and it begins with understanding.

We *can* do it if each of us will see clearly that he plays more than one role in our economy. I invite every American—regardless of his economic status—to look into what I visualize as a three-way mirror of good citizenship in which our over-all well-being is reflected.

First of all, everyone sees himself as a consumer. That's obvious from a straight-ahead look in the citizenship mirror. Then, by looking simultaneously in one of the mirror's side panels, some seventy million of us who are employed can see ourselves not only as consumers but also as producers or earners. Of these, some 17½ million are members of labor unions.

In the mirror's other side panel, about 120 million of us are reflected. These are all the investors, thanks to the savings made possible by our American abundance which yields discretionary income—money above and beyond what we need just to live. More than a hundred million are indirect shareowners through a variety of financial institutions such as mutual savings banks, insurance companies, pension funds, and so on. Sixteen and a half million adults— very close to the number belonging to unions—are stockholders in American corporations.

Those of us who limit their visions to any one of the three panels of the citizenship mirror see only a pocketbook issue. And this accounts for the great apathy toward the infinitely more important over-all issues—the national interest issues having to do with our very economic survival. . . .

Despite the fact that profits are generally regarded as merely something left over after consumption has been taken care of by production, that's not the way our economy works. Profits are vital to investment, and we must invest before we can produce and we must produce before we can consume.

Our economy moves forward only when both the investors' money and the workers' labor are combined efficiently to produce profitably what the consumer wants. This combination must provide:

Prices that represent value to the consumer

The wherewithal for good wages for the worker

An adequate reward for the investor for risking his funds

And—of great importance—the capital so necessary for business expansion. . . .

The simple truth, as we all know, is that profits—and only profits—provide the incentive for investors to continue investing and that undistributed earnings must be available for ploughing back in the interests of keeping business modern and growing.

Unfortunately, John Q. Public is far more concerned about holding prices down and getting more wages for himself. He is not at all concerned about the level of corporate profits because he is looking into only one panel of the citizenship mirror. He does not understand that the favorable level of price he pays for a wanted item has frequently been made possible by the efficiency of the machines which made it. Nor does he grasp that it is only a *sufficient* profit which has made it possible to buy modern machines to replace obsolete ones.

**NEW HORIZONS
IN ECONOMICS**

Abridged from "New Horizons in Economics" by Robert L. Heilbroner from *Saturday Review* (August 29, 1964). Reprinted by permission of the author and *Saturday Review*.

1 Who are the "bypassed members of our society"?
2 In what ways are unemployment figures in the United States unrealistic?
3 What suggestions does Heilbroner have for finding work for the unemployed?
4 What is the author's "new frontier" of employment?

It is curious how rapidly economic fashions change. A few years ago the economic word *en vogue* was affluence, and the problems economists talked about were those of abundance and leisure. Today we hear instead about the twenty, forty, or seventy million Americans who are poor, depending on whether we define poverty as subsistence, adequacy, or minimal comfort. One would think from the trend of public concern that the country must have been declining in the intervening years. Yet, for all our current preoccupation with poverty, average incomes have risen by an eighth over the past five years, and we are appreciably more affluent a society than in 1958, when J. K. Galbraith's influential book [*The Affluent Society*] was written. To take a figure that I find astonishing, one-quarter of all nonfarm families have now crossed over the $10,000 income line, and nearly half of them over the $7,500 line.

To talk of poverty in the face of such statistics is to risk appearing to be a professional hypochondriac. Yet there is a reason to accent the negative, even in the face of such positive indications. For the forces that are exerting their powerful hydraulic lift do not operate equally—nor even equitably—on all sections of the American public alike. Some are by passed. Worse yet, some are actually pulled downward in the backwash of the forces of propulsive momentum.

The bypassed portion of our society is one which we have become sporadically aware of throughout our history; we are in such a spasm of recognition at the moment. For it became clear during the great boom of the 1950s that currents of the great stream of purchasing power barely penetrate into certain reaches of the American economy, whose poverty remains stubbornly undissolved by the general prosperity. The old, eking out their days on a stingy Social Security allowance (62 per cent of all income recipients over age 65 get less than $1000 a year total income); the Negro family condemned by discrimination to an average standard of living that totals only 52 per cent of white earnings; the family struggling along without a male earner (at the same income disadvantage as the nonwhite); the Mississippi farmer who makes only a fourth as much as a California farmer; and the Appalachian family on relief who may receive only a fourth as much as a Mississippi farmer—these are the "pockets" of poverty that defy the general advance. They do not defy it entirely; bit by bit the stagnant backwaters are drawn out into the main channel. But the pace is agonizingly slow.

Hence, if we are looking into the economic future, we shall have to count the not-so-newly poor side by side with the newly affluent. But this static sector is not what is most disturbing about the prospects ahead. Much more unsettling, because it is much more dynamic, is a problem about whose implications we are still loath to think clearly. This is the re-emergence of unemployment in the midst of the longest sustained climb the economy has ever known, and, more serious yet, the possibility that this unemployment is the sign of a fundamental challenge to which nothing less than the opening of a new frontier will be the answer.

We are still unused to the extent of this unemployment and reluctant to tally it fully. There is a considerable temptation to dismiss the unemployment problem as affecting "only" about 5.5 per cent of the labor force, compared with an unemployment rate of 4.5 per cent in the boom years from 1947 to 1957. A gain of one percentage point does not seem unduly alarming, even after we have been told that it means an increase of 1,000,000 in the number of men and women unable to find work.

But this is still only the "visible" unemployed—those who declare to the Department of Labor poll-takers that they are actively looking for work and cannot get it. To these 4,200,000 visibly jobless during 1963 we must add another 2,300,000 who sought full-time work but could get only part-time work. And even that is not the full count. There are in addition an indeterminate number, estimated at perhaps 2,000,000, who do not declare themselves "unemployed" to the poll-taker because they have simply stopped looking for work. Many lower-income housewives, for instance, would work if there were work to be had, but because they know that a search for a job is likely to be fruitless they stay at home.

Hence, there is reason to be concerned over the unemployment situation, even though on the surface it is not "bad." For if we add to the official unemployment rate of 5.7 per cent for 1963 the unemployment represented by part-time work and by stay-at-homes, we get a total rate that is very close to 10 per cent. Ten per cent of the labor force is still very far away from the terrible days of the Depression, when an equivalent calculation would have revealed a rate of at least 30 per cent. But it is sizable enough to represent a cause for deep concern.

How can we account for this slowly worsening problem at a time when so many in the nation have been experiencing a continuous prosperity?

It is usual to place the blame on the fact that our total dollar output, our Gross National Product, has not been growing fast enough. And it is true enough that our rate of growth of dollar output since 1958 is slower by perhaps a third than pre-1958. It is also true that if we could find ways of making our rate of growth increase considerably—let us say to the level of Western Europe or of the USSR—we would undoubtedly find jobs for many million more Americans. And yet talk about the rate of growth in some ways obscures rather than clarifies the problem. For it hides the crucial fact that one of the main causes for such growth as we do have is also a primary cause for the unemployment we are suffering. That double-acting cause—both adding to our rate of output and subtracting from our rate of employment—is the extraordinary technology of the late 1950s and early 1960s, a technology to which we have given the name "automation.". . .

. . . To some extent, . . . automation is only a continuation of the past—a thrust of new techniques that will push men from field to factory and from factory to office. But the new technology, with its humanoid sensory devices and its uncanny capacities to "learn" and to correct and guide itself, has an additional potentiality as well. For the first time it threatens to invade the office as well—*to mechanize the service and administrative branches of work and thereby to bring to an end their steady growth as a source of work.* Anyone who has visited a modern bank or insurance company or corporate office and seen batteries of silent computers and clunking electric printers do the work of file clerks and shipping clerks and bookkeepers and office managers has seen this new technology in action. What he has also seen is the belated entry of technology into the last major field of economic activity, where it will once again play the role it has already performed in agriculture and industry. This time, however, where shall our unneeded labor go?

There remains one last twist to the problem. The new service-performing technology in itself poses a substantial enough threat to our economy. But to make matters worse, it is cutting into our employment base, both on the factory floor and in the office, at the very time when requirements for new jobs are reaching record heights. The huge crop of one-time war babies, having burst through the nation's high schools and inundated its colleges, is about to emerge onto the market place for jobs. By way of giving some idea of how many jobs will be needed, consider that between 1950 and 1960 the young labor force, aged fourteen to twenty-four, increased by half a million. Between 1960 and 1970 it will increase by 6,000,000.

Already we can feel the first effects of this rapidly expanding labor supply. Last year the jobless rate among white teen-agers looking for work was 15.6 per cent. Among nonwhite teen-agers it was 30 per cent. And the full impact is yet to come.

Automation is not, of course, the only economic problem of the future. No one can look ten and twenty years ahead without asking worried questions about disarmament and its impact on our over-militarized economic machine; about our relations with the underdeveloped world, at once so inescapable and so frustrating; about our growing competitive struggle with Europe; about affluence itself, with its prospects for an orgy of commercialism, a Saturnalia of advertising. Yet in many ways the problem of automation lies at the center of things, not alone in its human impact but in the larger implications of its challenge.

That challenge is to find a new frontier of employment to take the place of the disappearance of the service sector, the last great expansive area of private employment. But where can this frontier be? Where can we still use the skills and strengths of millions of Americans, some trained and some not, some young and some not so young? If one asks the question seriously, it is not difficult to answer it. America cries out for work to be done. The cities, ugly and rotten, must be rebuilt. The schools, still fearfully inadequate to their all-important task, must be expanded. The recreational space of the nation, cramped and undermanned, must be enlarged. The growing numbers of the old must be given homes, even villages, with nurses and companions. The public safety and the public convenience, both shockingly neglected in America, must be attended to. And not least, the poor must be guided out of their poverty and, where that is not possible, at least given the dignity of adequate support.

So there is no dearth of wants, no satiety of needs, no lack of work that might be done. But—and this is the crucial thing—all these wants and needs and employments will have to be initiated and financed and supported by the public sector. These are not goods or services that the market can provide. They are, without exception, matters that the community will provide through its public agencies, or that the community will not have. There is more here than just a series of remedial measures to provide some necessary jobs. The provision of the public well-being represents, I believe, the next stage of economic activity to which a society naturally turns once it has begun to fulfil the demands of the private well-being. This is not to say that the sphere of private wants will not grow or that the private sector will not remain dominant in our economic life. But the challenge of the future does not seem to me to lie any longer in the private zone. It is the public zone that is still small and mean and dingy and poor—and increasingly important. Here is where the horizons are big.

Whether we shall meet this challenge with boldness it is difficult to say. Without doubt we shall hear the cry that it is social-ism and the warning that the expansion of the public facilities will destroy the remaining vestiges of our personal liberties. But we can also be certain that the impersonal forces of the economy will be pushing us steadily into the new terrain where human labor, in its traditional places of work, becomes ever more redundant. . . . It is enough to brace ourselves for what is likely to be the central contro-versy of American political and economic life for at least the next decade and maybe more.

**THE THEORY OF
SOCIAL BALANCE**

Copyright © 1958 by John Kenneth Galbraith. Reprinted by permission of the publisher, Houghton Mifflin Company.

1 What does "social balance" have to do with slicing the economic pie?
2 Exactly what is Galbraith criticizing?

In the years following World War II, the papers of any major city . . . told daily of the shortages and shortcomings in the elemen-tary municipal and metropolitan services. The schools were old and overcrowded. The police force was under strength and underpaid. The parks and playgrounds were insufficient. Streets and empty lots were filthy, and the sanitation staff was underequipped and in need of men. Access to the city by those who work there was uncertain and painful and becoming more so. Internal transportation was overcrowded, unhealthful, and dirty. So was the air. Parking on the streets had to be prohibited, and there was no space elsewhere. These deficiencies were not in new and novel services but in old and established ones. . . .

The discussion of this public poverty competed, on the whole successfully, with the stories of ever-increasing opulence in privately produced goods. The Gross National Product was rising. So were retail sales. So was personal income. Labor productivity had also advanced. The automobiles that could not be parked were being produced at an expanded rate. The children, though without schools, . . . were admirably equipped with television sets. We had difficulty finding storage space for the great surpluses of food despite a national disposition to obesity. Food was grown and packaged under private auspices. The care and refreshment of the mind, in contrast with the stomach, was principally in the public domain. Our colleges and universities were severely overcrowded and underprovided, and the same was true of the mental hospitals.

The contrast was and remains evident not alone to those who read. The family which takes its mauve and cerise, air-conditioned, power-steered, and power-braked automobile out for a tour passes through cities that are badly paved, made hideous by litter, blighted buildings, billboards, and posts for wires that should long since have been put underground. They pass on into a countryside that has been rendered largely invisible by commercial art. . . . They picnic on exquisitely packaged food from a portable icebox by a polluted stream. . . . Just before dozing off on an air mattress, beneath a nylon tent, amid the stench of decaying refuse, they may reflect vaguely on the curious unevenness of their blessings. Is this, indeed, the American genius? . . .

Just as there must be balance in what a community produces, so there must also be balance in what the community consumes. . . . If we are to consume more automobiles, we must have more gasoline. There must be more insurance as well as more space on which to operate them. Beyond a certain point more and better food appears to mean increased need for medical services. . . .

However, the relationships we are here discussing are not confined to the private economy. They operate comprehensively over the whole span of private and public services. As surely as an increase in the output of automobiles puts new demands on the steel industry so, also, it places new demands on public services. Similarly, every increase in the consumption of private goods will normally mean some facilitating or protective step by the state. In all cases if these services are not forthcoming, the consequences will be in some degree ill. It will be convenient to have a term which suggests a satisfactory relationship between the supply of privately produced goods and services and those of the state, and we may call it social balance. . . .

The city of Los Angeles, in modern times, is a near-classic study in the problem of social balance. Magnificently efficient factories and oil refineries, a lavish supply of automobiles, a vast consumption of handsomely packaged products, coupled with the absence of a municipal trash collection service which forced the use of home incinerators, made the air nearly unbreathable for an appreciable part of each year. Air pollution could be controlled only by a complex and highly developed set of public services—by better knowledge stemming from more research, better policing, a municipal trash collection service, and possibly the assertion of the priority of clean air over the production of goods. These were long in coming. The agony of a city without usable air was the result.

The issue of social balance can be identified in many other current problems. Thus an aspect of increasing private production is the appearance of an extraordinary number of things which lay claim to the interest of the young. Motion pictures, television, automobiles, and the vast opportunities which go with the mobility, together with such less enchanting merchandise as narcotics, comic books, and pornographia, are all included in an advancing gross national product. . . .

In a well-run and well-regulated community, with a sound school system, good recreational opportunities, and a good police force—in short a community where public services have kept pace with private production—the diversionary forces operating on the modern juvenile may do no great damage. Television and the violent mores of Hollywood and Madison Avenue must contend with the intellectual discipline of the school. The social, athletic, dramatic, and like attractions of the school also claim the attention of the child. These, together with the other recreational opportunities of the community, minimize the tendency to delinquency. Experiments with violence and immorality are checked by an effective law-enforcement system before they become epidemic.

In a community where public services have failed to keep abreast of private consumption things are very different. Here, in an atmosphere of private opulence and public squalor, the private goods have full sway. Schools do not compete with television and the movies. The dubious heroes of the latter, not Miss Jones, become the idols of the young. . . .

Moreover, in a society which sets large store by production, and which has highly effective machinery for synthesizing private wants, there are strong pressures to have as many wage earners in the family as possible. As always all social behavior is part of a piece. If both parents are engaged in private production, the burden on the public services is further increased. Children, in effect, become the charge of the community for an appreciable part of the time. If the services of the community do not keep pace, this will be another source of disorder.

Residential housing also illustrates the problem of the social balance, although in a somewhat complex form. Few would wish to contend that, in the lower or even the middle-income brackets, Americans are munificently supplied with housing. A great many families would like better located or merely more houseroom, and no advertising is necessary to persuade them of their wish. And the provision of housing is in the private domain. At first glance at least, the line we draw between private and public seems not to be preventing a satisfactory allocation of resources to housing.

On closer examination, however, the problem turns out to be not greatly different from that of education. It is improbable that the housing industry is greatly more incompetent or inefficient in the United States than in . . . countries . . . where slums have been largely eliminated . . . . As the experience of these countries shows, . . . the housing industry functions well only in combination with a large, complex, and costly array of public services.

The case for social balance has, so far, been put negatively. Failure to keep public services in minimal relation to private production and use of goods is a cause of social disorder or impairs economic performance. The matter may now be put affirmatively. By failing to exploit the opportunity to expand public production we are missing opportunities for enjoyment which otherwise we might have had. Presumably a community can be as well rewarded by buying better schools or better parks as by buying bigger automobiles. By concentrating on the latter rather than the former it is failing to maximize its satisfactions. As with schools in the community, so with public services over the country at large. It is scarcely sensible that we should satisfy our wants in private goods with reckless abundance, while in the case of public goods, on the evidence of the eye, we practice extreme self-denial. So, far from systematically exploiting the opportunities to derive use and pleasure from these services, we do not supply what would keep us out of trouble.

THE UNJOINED DEBATE

Abridgment of "The Unjoined Debate" by George Stigler from *Chicago Today* (Winter 1966). Reprinted by permission of *Chicago Today* and the author, Dr. George Stigler, Charles R. Walgreen Distinguished Service Professor in the Department of Economics and the Graduate School of Business.

1 Why does the author feel that economic liberals and conservatives are not addressing themselves properly to issues?
2 Why is the subject of "liberty" not a viable or pertinent subject of controversy?
3 How may an economic conservative be "humane" and still object to certain forms of public welfare programs?

The controversy between conservatives and liberals in the United States is so ineffective that it is not serving the purposes of controversy. The quality of controversy is not only low but in fact declining, and what was once a meaningful debate is becoming completely unjoined. An unjoined debate is only an affront to the social intelligence. I intend to blame both parties for this failure, and I seek to contribute to their confrontation on several basic issues. Since I am undoubtedly conservative, and only hopefully fairminded, you should be warned against that perennial and not always intentional gambit, the restatement of an issue in such a way that it has only one defensible side. . . .

Let us begin with the most fundamental issue posed by the increasing direction of economic life by the state: the preservation of the individual's liberty—liberty of speech, of occupation, of choice of home, of education.

The situation is presently this: Everyone agrees that liberty is important and desirable; hardly anyone believes that any basic liberties are seriously infringed today. The conservatives believe that a continuation of the trend toward increasing political control over economic life will inevitably lead to a larger diminution of liberty. The liberals believe that this contingency is remote and avoidable. The more mischievous of the liberals point out that the conservatives have been talking of the planting of the seeds of destruction of liberty for decades—perhaps the seeds are infertile. Liberty is thus not a viable subject of controversy; neither side takes the issue seriously. . . .

A second striking failure of communication is the problem of individual welfare.

The academic conservative is dedicated to an efficient price system. This price system will direct resources to their most important uses, weed out inefficient entrepreneurs, induce improvements in technology, and otherwise contribute to a large national product. Many so-called welfare programs interfere with the workings of this price system and are opposed by the conservative. A minimum wage law is a direct interference with this price system in the market for labor services, and wheat subsidies are a similar interference in the market for foodstuffs—and the conservative says both interferences should be stopped.

To the liberal the conservative's preoccupation with efficiency seems outrageous. The liberal sees a numerous family supported by an ill-paid wage earner, and asserts that an economy as rich as ours can afford to pay a meager $1.25 or $2.00 an hour to this wage-earner. The liberal saw a farm family bankrupted in 1933 by the collapse of our economy, and feels that no legitimate purpose is served by again subjecting farmers to hurricanes of economic adversity. A well-bred liberal will not openly voice his doubts of the benevolence of a conservative but it is difficult to believe that the liberal does not suspect that the conservative has greater love for profits than for people.

I venture to assert that the conservative is an earnest friend of man but that he looks at welfare in a less personal and restricted way than the liberal. When the price of wheat is raised by a crop restriction scheme, everyone can observe the benefit to the owner of the farm, and it is this benefit that catches the liberal eye. The conservative is troubled by two other effects of the crop restriction scheme: A tax has been levied on all the consumers of bread; and the restriction scheme almost inevitably will lead to some waste of resources or, differently put, reduce the community's real income. These effects are obviously harmful to non-farmers. The conservative's opposition to minimum wage legislation is more direct: Such legislation injures some of the lowest paid workers by forcing them into even lower paid occupations exempt from the act, one of which is unemployment.

The conservative's preference for low prices, strong incentives to diligence and thrift and inventiveness, and similar attributes of efficiency and progress, has indeed a substantial advantage over the liberal's plan of assisting particular needy groups. There are many, many needy groups in a society, and some take a generation or two or even three before they catch the eye of the liberal, be he reformer or politician. The liberal started to care for the poorly housed in American cities a few years ago. In the preceding 300 years the private enterprise economy had sole responsibility for improving their housing. The liberal hopes to take especially good care of the poverty-stricken in Appalachia in 1966—notice the date; but he will ignore the dozens of other groups of equal or greater need until someone publicizes their need. The conservative's programs are designed to help everyone, groups too poor to have a press agent.

These remarks are intended to illustrate a general proposition: The conservative opposition to intervention by either government or private monopoly is commonly stated in efficiency terms but could always be restated in terms of welfare, and especially in the welfare of consumers. A conservative may be truly humane. It is fair to say that the conservative is compassionate for the great mass of the population which is moderately affected by each public policy, whereas the liberal is compassionate for the special, identifiable group which is most benefited or injured by the policy in question. . . .

But there is more than this to the conservative position. Suppose we wish to help a particular group of farmers or slum dwellers or a disaster-stricken community. Often it is possible—in fact, usually it is possible—to devise policies which impose a minimum of harm on other groups, or place this harm on a known group capable of bearing it. In our example of the farm program, for example, we can choose between direct income grants that do not lead to a waste of resources or—as at present—a crop restriction scheme that does waste resources. We can finance the benefits to farmers by charging more for bread, or by using general tax revenues. I may add that no economist who is outside active politics will defend the present farm program, whether he be liberal or conservative.

I shall be so absurdly fair-minded as to notice the reply to this discussion by a fair-minded liberal. True, he will say, too little attention has been devoted by us liberals to the effects of our policies on people who cannot afford to send a representative to the congressional committee hearings. We grant you conservatives humanity and shall reckon indirect effects of our policies henceforth. But do you deny that conservatives opposed social security, all farm programs, the urban renewal programs, the recent anti-poverty bill, etc.? Have not the conservatives been *too* preoccupied with the indirect and diffused costs of programs to give due weight to their direct and immediate benefits for hard-hit groups?

On reflection I am inclined to give two answers. The first is that the rise of per capita incomes (in 1964 prices) from about $500 in 1875 to $2000 today is a measure of the immense benevolence implicit in a private enterprise system, and this rise has not only done more to eliminate poverty than all governmental policies ever devised, but has in fact also financed these policies. The second answer is, touché.

QUESTIONS FOR CLOSER STUDY

1 Is the dispute over *who* should slice the economic pie or *how* it should be sliced?

2 Should private enterprise be obligated to share its profits

with labor and society? Why or why not?

3 What should be the role of industry in helping to clear up pollution and slum conditions and to alleviate poverty? What should be the role of government?

4 Do you find evidence in these selections of criticism of American values as well as of unequal wealth distribution? How is the American system defended?

5 Defend or attack the following statement: "That economic philosophy is best which brings about the greatest good for the greatest number of people."

CHAPTER 6

HOW
SHOULD WAGES
BE DETERMINED

According to modern economic theory, wages are determined by the demand for and supply of various kinds of labor. However, this interaction of supply and demand is affected by collective bargaining, wage legislation, and other such institutional arrangements which help to shape the wage bargain struck between employer and employee.

This chapter is designed to acquaint the reader with several issues in wage determination. Because of the wide range of jobs in the United States, it is impossible to simply and concisely answer the question "How are wages determined?" An electrician is paid an hourly wage by custom, but a TV entertainer can insist on a weekly or annual contract. A professional football player can negotiate a salary based on his record, but an elevator operator must be paid at least a minimum wage set by law.

Because workers in different occupations have different skills and needs, they have demanded that wages be determined in a number of ways. In recent years, companies and their employees have negotiated wages mostly of the basis of three criteria: 1) cost-of-living indexes, 2) productivity indicators, and 3) wage guidelines, establishing both minimum and maximum wages.

The authors of the selections in this chapter define and discuss these criteria, revealing strong differences over how wages should be determined—from strict legislative controls at one extreme to a free market at the other. In doing so, they indicate their views about wage determination in general. The real question, then, centers as much on whether or not wage determinants should be legislated as on which criterion for wage determination should prevail.

The AFL-CIO explained its reasons for favoring the use of productivity as a basis for wage determination in an article that appeared in the November 1963 issue of the *AFL-CIO American Federationist*. The first selection is taken from that article.

In the second reading, Brown University economics professor Philip Taft discusses the usefulness of productivity guidelines in maintaining consumer purchasing power without creating inflation. Professor Taft's article originally appeared in the April 1963 issue of *Challenge* as a reaction to the Kennedy administration's proposal to establish wage guidelines.

The third selection is taken from *Minimum Wage Laws*, a bulletin published in 1961 by the New York State School of Industrial and Labor Relations at Cornell University. Written by Cornell economics professor Donald E. Cullen, it discusses favorable aspects of minimum wage laws.

Yale Brozen, professor of business economics at the University of Chicago, and Milton Friedman, professor of economics at the same university, reacted strongly to a bill presented to Congress early in 1966 to raise the minimum wage. They held that minimum wage legislation did not achieve its intended effect. The fourth reading is taken from their article which was published in April 1966 by the Free Society Association, Inc.

The fifth selection, by A. H. Raskin, assistant editor of the editorial page of *The New York Times*, was published in the February 10, 1968, issue of *Saturday Review*. Raskin discusses profit-sharing as an alternative to more traditional wage determinants.

**SOARING PRODUCTIVITY:
A FAIR SHARE
FOR LABOR**

Abridged from "Soaring Productivity: A Fair Share for Labor" from AFL-CIO AMERICAN FEDERATIONIST (November 1963). Reprinted by permission of American Federation of Labor and Congress of Industrial Organizations.

1 What has hampered growth in production in the author's opinion?
2 What could be some consequences of not basing wages on productivity?
3 Do you agree that education and other government expenditures increase productivity? Why or why not?

The meaning of the word "productivity" is quite simple. At one time or another, most people check the performance of their car by determining the number of miles they can travel per gallon of gasoline. The results give some indication of how efficiently the car is performing.

Similarly, productivity is a measure of the efficiency with which we produce goods and services. Instead of miles per gallon of gasoline, we measure such efficiency most frequently in terms of how much can be produced by the labor of one person during one hour— that is, in terms of output per manhour.

Thus if we add the value (after eliminating the effect of price changes) of all the goods and services produced throughout the private part of our economy and divide the sum by all the manhours of work which it took to produce those goods and services, we can determine output per manhour for the total private economy. As a result of such calculations, it is possible to say that the average employee in private industry produced 3.9 percent more goods and services in one hour in 1962 than in 1961. . . .

Increases in output per manhour are the result of the decisions and actions of a great many people and a great many organizations. Management, labor, consumers and society in general have all contributed in some way to such increases. . . .

A number of economists have even concluded that the development of our human resources through education and other government expenditures has contributed far more to the growth in output per manhour than our investment in plant and equipment. . . .

Workers also have contributed much to the growth in productivity in their capacity as producers and as members of trade union organizations. They have invested considerable time and effort in acquiring greater knowledge and skill. They have also been quite willing to accept changes in work methods and have frequently suggested such changes themselves. And through their trade unions they have frequently assisted and often prodded less efficient firms into becoming more efficient. Prevented by union action from lowering wages . . . , many firms have had to devise more efficient methods of production in order to lower costs and remain competitive.

Management has made significant contributions to productivity also. These have generally taken the form of investment in new plant and equipment, expenditures on research and development and more effective methods of administering business and selling products.

The fact is that productivity gains result from a complex interaction of factors for which labor and society as a whole, as well as management, are responsible. No one group can claim all the credit for the steady increases in productivity which we have enjoyed and no one group is, therefore, entitled to all the benefits which flow from such increases. As individuals, as members of trade unions and as citizens supporting and promoting a variety of government activities, workers have contributed to the growth in productivity and therefore have an unquestionable moral right to share in its fruits along with management and other groups. . . .

Rising productivity means that we can produce as much or even more than before with fewer workers. Yet a growing labor force means more people seeking work than ever before. Obviously, unless hours of work are shortened, production and sales must grow rapidly enough to make up for the jobs which the growth in productivity would otherwise destroy and to create additional jobs for new workers as well. . . .

. . . The growth in the labor force and the increase in output per manhour have made it possible and necessary to increase production at a yearly rate of 4 percent to 4.5 percent since 1953. However, production and sales have been expanding at the much slower rate of 2.8 percent. . . .

The slow growth in demand is not likely to be reversed, however, unless business shares the benefits of increasing productivity with other groups in society. Consumers are the main source of demand. They purchase about 70 percent of all the goods and services we produce. But they are able to do so, for the most part, only because of the income they receive from wages and salaries.

Obviously, if wages fail to rise sufficiently while profits and dividends and other forms of income increase disproportionately, consumer demand for goods and services will lag. Wealth will become concentrated in the hands of those who tend to save much of their income or to invest it. And the result, inevitably, will be a further widening in the gap between our ability to produce and our ability to consume.

CAN 'GUIDELINES' SOLVE THE PROBLEM?

Abridgment of "Can 'Guidelines' Solve the Problem?" by Philip Taft from Challenge (April 1963). Reprinted by permission of Challenge, The Magazine of Economic Affairs, a publication of Challenge Communications, Inc.

1 What were the purposes of the Kennedy administration's proposal to place a limit on wage increases?
2 How could establishing guidelines alter the role of government in labor relations in peacetime? Why does the author consider this new role impractical?
3 How does the author think that the application of wage guidelines might alter the political activity of labor union members?

For a long time businessmen, labor union officials, clergymen and politicians have sought to discover the perfect wage formula which would be just and equitable and would promote economic growth and human harmony. This quest, of course, can never be completely successful. But neither can it be said that the United States has failed in its endeavor to set equitable wage standards. . . .

In the absence of a central wage policy devised jointly by union and employer organizations, such as prevails in Sweden, the Kennedy Administration proposed that wage raises be limited to the average national increase in productivity, or about three per cent a year. The Administration hoped that such a limit on wage increases would lead to the stabilization of prices. This in turn would eliminate the danger of inflation and would enhance the competitiveness of American exports. . . .

Although it seems that the suggested standards for limiting wage increases or guidelines, as they are called, are not as rigid as appeared at first, the very idea of a formula raises several questions. Are wage guidelines practical, and if so, desirable? . . .

For many years labor and management have agreed on new contracts in free negotiations. While the results have not been perfect, the nation has enjoyed high prosperity and a rising gross national product in the postwar period. Perhaps the United States economy could and should do better, but the lag in performance cannot be attributed to an absence of guidelines. Of course, the government has intervened in a number of negotiations in crucial industries and has influenced the final outcome. Nevertheless, no attempt was made to establish in advance a standard which labor and management were obligated to accept. Consequently, the establishment of guidelines which would set a ceiling on wage increases would substantially alter the role of government in labor relations in peacetime.

If annual guidelines are to be more than meaningless pronouncements, the government would have to exert direct or indirect pressure to force their acceptance. However, the measurements of productivity upon which guidelines are based are not sufficiently precise to serve as a basis for wage settlements. . . .

In any one year some industries are likely to increase productivity at a more rapid rate than others. Also productivity is declining in some ailing industries while it is rising in others. In addition, rates of productivity growth vary even among enterprises in a particular industry. New plants are likely to increase productivity at a faster annual rate than older ones in the same industry. And, of course, through exceptional ability, the management of a particular firm may enhance the productivity rise.

In view of these differences, it is obviously inequitable to compel all firms to follow the same wage increase policies. . . . Consequently, the insistence that guidelines set a limit on wage increases rather than guarantee a specific rate of increase is for practical purposes less significant than is often assumed. . . .

The use of guidelines also tends to make the government a party to all wage negotiations. Thousands of wage rates are negotiated by labor and management quietly and without fanfare. If the guideline policy were to be effective, a check would have to be maintained on all negotiations. . . . To avoid penalizing firms which are in the focus of public attention, a new system of reporting and news control would have to be instituted. Otherwise, less-well-known firms could evade compliance.

Guidelines would also make collective bargaining more difficult and would, in fact, increase inflationary pressures within the economy. Once labor became thoroughly aware of this guiding principle of wage adjustments workers and their unions would press more insistently for employer concessions. . . .

The application of guidelines would, however, prevent, or at least decrease, the opportunity of workers to gain more than limited raises if their company's profits are high. . . .

Wage guidelines imply at least some control over the prices of goods and services. But the government could not impose its price standards equally upon all segments of the economy. Large firms with few competitors might be more easily pressured into holding the price line than medium-sized or smaller firms. Moreover, a policy of controlling prices in a free economy is enmeshed in insoluble problems. . . .

Experience with wage controls during World War II showed that government fixing of wages tends to introduce a political element into collective bargaining. Political pressures are inevitably applied to obtain special consideration for one or both parties in a negotiation. Guidelines based on average changes in productivity cannot be sufficiently clear . . . to make them . . . [a] standard for wage setting. . . .

In contrast to legislation regulating collective bargaining, such as the Wagner and Taft-Hartley Acts, or measures regulating internal union affairs, like the Landrum-Griffin Act, government involvement in wage setting would directly affect virtually every worker. In other words, it would be easier for a union leader to show workers that government policy determined the size of their pay envelopes. Thereby the active involvement of the rank and file in politics would be encouraged. Workers might contribute more readily to campaign funds raised by labor unions if their pay checks were affected by the election results.

The employer, on the other hand, is not prohibited by the guideline principle from refusing labor's demands. The rule merely places a ceiling on the level of his concessions, although it might incidentally make bargaining and recruitment of labor more difficult. The faithful carrying out of wage guideline directives might stimulate the political consciousness of labor to a far greater extent than "prolabor" or "antilabor" legislation could in the past.

But it is far more likely that the guidelines will soon be forgotten. . . .

All these, and many other hotly debated economic slogans and ideas of today, will soon pass into oblivion.

MINIMUM WAGE LAWS

Abridged from MINIMUM WAGE LAWS, Bulletin 43 by Donald E. Cullen. Published by New York State School of Industrial and Labor Relations. Reprinted by permission of the author.

1 According to some analysts, how do minimum wage laws depress some wages and contribute to unemployment?
2 What arguments does Cullen use to support minimum wage legislation?
3 According to the author, why is it difficult to generalize about the effects of minimum wage legislation?

Several detailed studies have been made of the impact of minimum wage laws, but different analysts view these studies from quite different perspectives. For instance, those who doubt the value of wage regulation expect the evidence to show that higher wages for some have been offset by unemployment, lower wages, or higher prices for others. This expectation springs not from malice but from a widely accepted belief as to how our economic system works. Assume, these critics suggest, that you are an employer now paying half your workers less than $1.00 an hour. What would you do if tomorrow you were ordered to pay everyone at least $1.00? You might absorb the resultant cost increase by reducing your profits, but your profits may be too small to permit this and, even if they are large, why shouldn't you try to retain them for yourself, your stockholders, or to reinvest in the business? To do this, or perhaps just to break even if you are particularly hard hit, you might raise your prices, although you know this will reduce your sales volume (and hence employment) or you would have raised them before this.

If competition is so stiff that you cannot raise prices, then you will probably seek to cut your unit costs back to their former level by increasing the output you obtain for every dollar of your wage bill. This might be done by using more labor-saving machinery, or raising work standards, or hiring better workers to replace the least efficient among your present force—all of which means unemployment for somebody, since today's level of output will thus be met tomorrow by fewer workers. Finally, if the workers you lay off were not "worth" $1.00 to you, they probably will not be worth that to other employers and will consequently have to seek work in low-wage industries not yet covered by a wage law—which will depress wages even further in those industries.

To all this, proponents of wage regulation say that it is small wonder that economics long ago earned the title of "the dismal science." They point out that nearly every type of welfare legislation has been opposed initially with the same predictions of disaster, predictions which they feel are based on the homely philosophy that the poor are always with us and for their own good it is best not to meddle with fate and free enterprise. Analysts of this persuasion turn to the impact studies in the knowledge that the country has not been ruined yet and therefore with the expectation of discovering that past minima have been absorbed quite easily. Their reasoning, which has achieved wide currency among economists specializing in labor problems, proceeds from three propositions.

First, as businessmen never tire of reminding economists, the real world is seldom as neatly ordered as theory implies. It is true that a competitive economy works quite well on the whole, but there is inevitably considerable slippage in a system as complex as our own. Workers can not shift about as easily as capital; unorganized workers are frequently at a disadvantage in bargaining with their employers; businessmen would be less than human if they always strained every fiber to operate at peak efficiency, even when under no pressure to do so.

For these and other reasons, it is argued that one cannot comfortably assume that in a free market all workers tend to be paid as much as the market can bear for their services. Many employers know they have some discretion in setting the wages they pay, for there would be no point to their many wage surveys and elaborate job-evaluation programs if market forces alone determined wage rates. Thus, there are great variations in the wages paid for the same type of labor in the same industry or the same city, and who is to say that the janitor paid $ .70 an hour on one side of town is not worth the $1.00 being paid the janitor on the other side of town? More to the point, who can safely predict that the first janitor will be laid off if he must be paid $1.00 an hour? Everyone has heard non-union employers predict complete bankruptcy if forced to accept a union, and yet most survive when organized and devise ways of living with the union scale short of wholesale layoffs. They may intensify their selling efforts, improve their plant layout, increase the training of their present workers and selection standards for new ones, strengthen the quality of supervision, and in these and other ways absorb most of the shock of a wage increase which first appeared ruinous.

Second, organized labor has long urged that wage increases be recognized as not only a cost increase for employers but also an increase in the purchasing power of consumers. Particularly in the case of low-wage workers, it is argued, increases are spent immediately—long before employers can undertake, for example, any large-scale substitution of machinery for labor—and they are usually spent in a way which directly benefits certain low-wage industries: through retail stores and for such products as food and clothing.

Third, the few employers truly unable to pay a decent wage should not be in business in the first place. To those who hold this view, it is both cruel and senseless to assert that the richest country on earth should do nothing about employers who today are unable to pay their workers $40 a week. If society really needs some of these employers in business, then let them be subsidized, not by their few workers in the form of low wages, but by society as a whole through any of the several forms of government aid already being given, for other reasons, to employers in many industries. If these employers are not essential, let their share of sales and their workers go to those who can pay a living wage. This is a harsh remedy for those affected and they should be given every aid possible in adjusting, but their numbers, it is said, will be small compared to those who directly benefit from a legal minimum.

. . . Since 1912 there have always been minimum wage laws in effect somewhere in the nation, for some states continued to enforce such laws even during the 1923-1937 period when they could not have withstood a court challenge. Yet, during the first forty years of this long experience, only twenty scattered studies were made which attempted to gather statistics on the actual effect of one or another of these laws, and many of these studies were not of high quality. It was not until 1955, seventeen years after the FLSA [Fair Labor Standards Act] was enacted, that Congress specifically directed the Secretary of Labor to supply it annually with data on the effects and adequacy of the act. Thus, until very recently the debate on this question has not been overburdened with facts. . . .

The essential reason why "the facts" on this question have proved inconclusive is that it is extremely difficult to separate out the effects of a legal minimum from the effects of dozens of other forces acting simultaneously in the economy. Changes in prices, wages, employment, and output are the result not only of changes in wage laws, but also of the interaction of shifting consumer tastes, management's investment decisions, the pattern of government taxing and spending, union activity, the discovery of new inventions, revolution in Cuba and recovery in Japan—the list is endless and, unfortunately for the analyst, none of these forces obligingly suspends operation when a new minimum wage is enacted. . . .

To sum up, the question of how workers and employers fare

under a minimum wage law is still unresolved, because (1) different people look at the evidence of past experience from quite different viewpoints, based on conflicting notions of how our economy operates, and (2) the evidence itself is so difficult to interpret that nearly everyone can point to some facts that appear to support his prior convictions.

**THE MINIMUM WAGE:
WHO PAYS?**

Abridged from "An Interview With Yale Brozen and Milton Friedman" from THE MINIMUM WAGE: WHO PAYS?. Reprinted by permission of The Free Society Association.

1 If you were a worker in a factory located where labor was cheap and transportation and equipment costs were high, would you be in favor of a high minimum wage? Why or why not?
2 If you were a skilled worker in a factory located where labor was expensive and transportation and equipment costs were low, would you be in favor of a high minimum wage? Why or why not?
3 How do you think Brozen and Friedman would reply to the contention that a high minimum wage affects sales of consumer goods?
4 What do you think Brozen and Friedman would say about the observation that U.S. employment has steadily increased since the passage of minimum wage legislation?

TO BEGIN WITH, WHO FAVORS SETTING MINIMUM WAGE RATES BY LAW—AND WHY?

FRIEDMAN. It's my impression that two very different groups favor minimum wage legislation. They may use the same arguments, but they are worlds apart in their motives.

One group has no special axe to grind. It's made up of well-meaning people who seem to believe that minimum wage legislation is truly in the general interest. They think, for example, that it contributes to reducing poverty—that a higher minimum wage rate means fewer people with low incomes. Or they think that it protects workers against exploitation, or raises the general level of purchasing power.

The other group has a very special axe to grind. It's the special interests—sometimes unions, sometimes managements, sometimes both in a particular region—who support increased minimum wage rates as a means of gaining a narrow advantage. For example, unions and managements in some northern industries—where wages will not be *directly* affected by the minimum because they're already well above it—favor national minimum wage laws in order to retard the movement of industry to the South. A good case in point is the New England textile industry. You see, one of the great inducements for industry, especially the textile industry, to move from New England to the South has been the possibility of hiring people at lower wages. So you find that people in this second group—and there are lots of them—favor higher minimum wage rates to prevent competition from developing in other parts of the country. And they don't make any bones about their position either. . . .

WHAT ABOUT THE ARGUMENT THAT THE MINIMUM WAGE HELPS WORKERS?

FRIEDMAN. It has some of the effects that its well-meaning supporters say it has. If the minimum wage rate is raised, *some* people's wages will go up. And this effect is very observable. You see a man whose wage is higher than it was before; he sees that his wage is higher, and he knows it's because of the increased minimum.

But the difficulty is that there are unseen, hidden effects that work in the opposite direction. Unquestionably, the most important effect of the minimum wage rate is unemployment. . . .

WHY DOES A HIKE IN THE MINIMUM WAGE RATE INCREASE UNEMPLOYMENT?

BROZEN. The higher rate will price some people right out of the market. It will make it too expensive for employers to hire certain categories of unskilled workers in certain jobs. So, plants will have to be closed. Or employers will begin to use more machinery or substitute supervisory and skilled employees for unskilled workers. People will be laid off. If they can't find new jobs in industries not covered by the minimum wage or learn new skills that make them worth more to employers, then the rate of unemployment will rise. . . .

ARE SOME GROUPS HURT MORE BY THE MINIMUM WAGE THAN OTHERS?

FRIEDMAN. Yes, indeed. Take Negro teenagers, for example. We all know the terrible social problems being caused, especially in our large cities, by the high rate of unemployment among Negro teen-

HOW SHOULD WAGES BE DETERMINED? **113**

agers. The fact is—it can be demonstrated statistically—the minimum wage rate is a major cause of Negro teenage unemployment. Of all the laws on the statute books of this country, I believe the minimum wage law probably does the Negroes the most harm. It is not intended to be an anti-Negro law but, in fact, it is. . . .

WHY ARE TEENAGERS IN GENERAL HURT MORE BY THE MINIMUM WAGE THAN ADULTS?

FRIEDMAN. If you had the choice of hiring an adult with experience and some skill or an inexperienced teenager—at the same wage rate —the odds are you'd hire the person with experience. So, clearly, what the minimum wage rate does is to take away from youngsters, and particularly from Negro youngsters, the one competitive advantage they have—the advantage of offering to work cheaper, in order to gain experience and to make a place for themselves.

IF IT IS SO CLEAR THAT THE MINIMUM WAGE DOES MORE HARM THAN GOOD, WHY DO SO MANY PEOPLE CONTINUE TO SUPPORT IT AND RECOMMEND INCREASES? IS IT SHEER IGNORANCE? . . .

FRIEDMAN. No, it's not ignorance. There is disagreement about the *extent* of these effects but I think most people realize that some of them, at least, do occur. However, this realization is countered by three things. First, the belief that the effects are small. Second, and much more important, the conviction that the additional unemployment, if there be some, either can be handled by new governmental efforts (neighborhood youth corps, job corps, public works programs)—or, more cynically, will bring the voters to support programs that the proponents really want anyway on other grounds.

BROZEN. As a matter of fact, Mr. Clarence Mitchell, director of the Washington bureau of the NAACP [National Association for the Advancement of Colored People], made pretty much this very point last year when he testified in favor of a $2.00 minimum wage. He admitted there was truth in the argument that a higher minimum would cause unemployment for many Negroes and young people, and said that that was why the NAACP also proposed "a national commitment to generate new jobs."

FRIEDMAN. Third—and this is a more sophisticated and difficult thing—there is the plain fact that the hardest thing in the world for a man to do is admit that he is wrong. Many people have come out in favor of the minimum wage rate. And now, even if they are persuaded of these effects, it's difficult for them to back down—as it would be for any of us.

PROFIT SHARING IN THE PAYCHECK

Abridged from "Profit Sharing in the Paycheck" by A. H. Raskin from SATURDAY REVIEW (February 10, 1968). Copyright Saturday Review, Inc. 1968. Reprinted by permission of the author and Saturday Review.

1 Why are unions now turning an about-face and asking for profit-sharing plans in industry?

2 How would deferred-payment profit-sharing plans put a break on run-away prices?

3 Does it seem that profit-sharing plans would demand legislated controls? Why or why not?

Collective bargaining has become a dog chasing its own tail, with inflation eating up wage increases before workers ever get a chance to spend them. Even the union leaders who bring home the fattest contracts these days are concluding that some new stabilizing element is needed to keep the extra purchasing power from draining out of their members' pay envelopes.

The welcome fruit of this discontent may be a growing concentration on wage plans geared to sharing efficiency. . . in place of the sterile "battle for the buck". . . .

There is, of course, nothing novel about the concept of giving workers a slice of corporate profits. . . . But most of the American plans up to now have been developed by employers who had no unions in their plants and wanted to keep things that way by increasing their employees' sense of identification with the business.

The interesting new element now is the extent to which the pressure for the introduction of profit sharing is coming from unions, with management in the objector role. Several factors, all of considerable relevance to the general problem of inflation control, help explain why unions in the basic industries are now pressing for a program they once fought as a prescription for union-busting or company unionism.

The most compelling of these factors, not surprisingly, is the enormous growth in industrial profits in the past seven years of uninterrupted boom. Even the slight shrinkage in earnings in some fields last year left overall profits so high that union leaders considered themselves shortchanged at the very time that they were pushing wages, pension, and fringes to record heights. The roller-coaster ups and downs of corporate earnings tended to dull the allure of profit-sharing schemes in the old days; but now unions, as ardent disciples of the "new economics," are beginning to believe that most billion-dollar corporations have become recession-proof.

A second factor is a widespread awareness at all levels in labor that the collapse of the Johnson Administration's wage-price guideposts has not erased the necessity for the kind of stability they were designed to promote. Nor has the guideposts' failure brought into question the soundness of their underlying thesis that the root of all real improvement in living standards for workers and everyone else lies in the improvement of national productivity. The more we produce, the more there is for all Americans to share. . . .

The union drive for profit sharing . . . had an unsuccessful trial run in the negotiations last fall between [Walter] Reuther's United Automobile Workers and the "Big Three" auto makers. The union called its plan "equity sharing," and put it forward not as a contract demand but as a proposal aimed at helping both sides break out of the pressure cooker of crisis bargaining.

The UAW statement to General Motors took note of perennial complaints that the union's wage demands would "do to death the golden goose." It suggested that giving workers a stake in above-average profits would introduce a new dimension into the argument over how much was enough by extending to them the same principle of compensation that determined the incomes of GM executives and stockholders.

Management's practice, the UAW noted, is to assign company officials a basic salary and then supplement it with bonuses based on the volume of GM's profits. Similarly, stockholders receive a regular dividend as a matter of course, to which extra dividends are added in years of special prosperity. "Why should this method of compensation not be applied to workers as well as to stockholders and executives?" the union asked. "Why should not workers receive,

in addition to their basic compensation reflecting the factors normally considered in negotiating wages and fringe benefits, a share in
the profits that their labor helps to create?"

The UAW came out of the 1967 negotiations with a bundle of
new gains—including the most substantial money package in its
three decades of bargaining—but equity sharing wound up in the
wastebasket. The very size of the settlement, however, and the upward push it has given to the spiral by exciting union appetites in
steel, aerospace, longshore, and other industries with contracts ex-
piring this year make it certain that the idea will not stay dead. . . .

The effectiveness of the profit-sharing approach as a brake
on runaway prices will be especially pronounced if future break-
throughs in union-negotiated plans are on the deferred-payment
basis that has marked most of the profit-sharing systems established
in this country since World War II. These programs assign the employee a nest egg to be taken in the form of an increased pension or
a lump-sum severance payment when he leaves the company. There
are tax advantages for both worker and employer in such arrangements; they reduce the disappointments that bad years bring when
workers start counting on profit sharing to pay family bills, and
they combat inflation by tamping down immediate demand. . . .

. . . [F]or employers, profit sharing has an advantage quite
apart from its impact on inflation and heightened employee interest
in making the business more prosperous. It encourages unions to set
basic wages for their industry on a more realistic level than they do
when the strongest company's ability to pay determines the contract
that everyone else must follow. This does not mean that unions will—
or should—accept a basic wage that fails to insure equity for all their
members, but it could rule out industry-wide standards so high that
they force all but the most efficient to shut up shop or merge with
the giants.

QUESTIONS FOR CLOSER STUDY

1 What is the problem most commonly expressed and at-
tacked by these authors?

2 Philip Taft asserts, "the measurements of productivity. . .
are not sufficiently precise to serve as a basis for wage settlements".

Why do you agree or disagree with this statement?

3 Do you think that Yale Brozen and Milton Friedman would accept any form of legislated wage determinants? Which one(s)? Why or why not?

4 What measures are mentioned in these readings that would defend the small businessman against big business, big unions, and big government? Do you think that it is right to consider small businessmen in debating wage determinants? Why or why not?

5 How do profit-sharing plans affect the strength of labor unions?

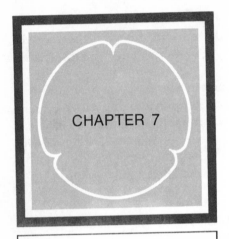

CHAPTER 7

SHOULD WE GUARANTEE INCOME

To what extent should a person be responsible for his economic needs? The variety of opinions on this question is represented at one extreme by those who insist that financial assistance from any level of government will inevitably result in the destruction of self-reliance. These people say that the resulting dependence on government aid will signal the emergence of a "welfare state" where each person is free not just from want but from responsibility as well.

At the opposite pole are those who derisively refer to the supporters of personal responsibility as advocates of a "jungle state". They believe that where there is no government assistance only the strongest men and women—or those with large inheritances—survive. The opinions of most Americans can be found somewhere between these extremes.

The controversy is revived each time welfare legislation is proposed. During the New Deal era [1933-1945] the introduction of social security, unemployment insurance, and subsidies to farmers represented an extension of government assistance to private citizens. Opponents insisted that these measures were economically unsound and morally indefensible. Those who defended the legislation contended that it provided built-in stabilizers that would prove to be economically beneficial to the entire economy. They also insisted that it was morally irresponsible for a government to ignore the needs of its citizens.

Today, acceptance of the principle of government responsibility for the poor has largely replaced the notion that to grant public assistance to needy people is to dignify poverty. Even among this majority, there is disagreement on specific questions. The definition of need is, at best, highly subjective; moreover, suggestions on how to alleviate poverty are nearly as numerous as people who make them. Americans are far from any national consensus on either of these issues.

When people of differing views attempt to arrive at an acceptable definition of poverty, they encounter considerable difficulty. Although it has been said that "a means test need not be mean", such a test, conducted to determine a family's economic need, is frequently considered distasteful by the people who are subjected to it.

The selections in this chapter discuss the "negative income tax" and the "guaranteed annual income". They are among the most recent proposals to expand the federal government's responsibility for the economic welfare of its citizens. They attempt to set minimum income standards and to provide for government payments to people with substandard incomes.

Professor Milton Friedman, an economist at the University

of Chicago, is generally considered as the originator of the negative income tax. The first reading is Friedman's statement describing his negative income tax proposal.

The second reading is by economist Robert Theobald. Theobald, in arguing for guaranteeing income, contends that every American citizen is entitled to an income that will enable him to live above the level of poverty.

Henry Hazlitt's article "The Coming Crisis in Welfare" was published in 1967. Directing his critique at Friedman, he discusses some of the weaknesses in Theobald's plan as well. Hazlitt is not opposed to society's accepting the responsibility for people who are "helpless . . . through no moral fault of their own", but he does not suggest how society *should be* responsible.

The fourth reading is by Sar A. Levitan, professor of economics at George Washington University. Published in May 1967, Levitan's article is an attack on both Friedman's and Theobald's proposals.

**THE ALLEVIATION
OF POVERTY**

"The Alleviation of Poverty." Reprinted from CAPITALISM AND FREEDOM by Milton Friedman, by permission of The University of Chicago Press. © 1962 by The University of Chicago Press.

1 According to Friedman, what are the advantages of a negative income tax?
2 If Friedman's proposal were adopted what effect do you think it would have on the unemployed people?
3 Does Friedman support existing relief and welfare measures? Why or why not?
4 What does Friedman believe is the major disadvantage of a negative income tax?

The extraordinary economic growth experienced by Western countries during the past two centuries and the wide distribution of the benefits of free enterprise have enormously reduced the extent of poverty in any absolute sense in the capitalistic countries of the West. But poverty is in part a relative matter, and even in these countries, there are clearly many people living under conditions that the rest of us label as poverty.

One recourse, and in many ways the most desirable, is private charity. . . .

It can be argued that private charity is insufficient because the benefits from it accrue to people other than those who make the gifts— . . . a neighborhood effect. I am distressed by the sight of poverty; I am benefited by its alleviation; but I am benefited equally whether I or someone else pays for its alleviation; the benefits of other people's charity therefore partly accrue to me. . . .

Suppose one accepts, as I do, this line of reasoning as justifying governmental action to alleviate poverty; to set, as it were, a floor under the standard of life of every person in the community. There remains the question, how much and how. . . .

Two things seem clear. First, if the objective is to alleviate poverty, we should have a program directed at helping the poor. There is every reason to help the poor man who happens to be a farmer, not because he is a farmer but because he is poor. The program, that is, should be designed to help people as people, not as members of particular occupational groups or age groups or wage-rate groups or labor organizations or industries. . . . Second, so far as possible the program should, while operating through the market, not distort the market or impede its functioning. This is a defect of price supports, minimum-wage laws, tariffs and the like.

The arrangement that recommends itself on purely mechanical grounds is a negative income tax. We now have an exemption of $600 per person under the federal income tax (plus a minimum 10 per cent flat deduction). If an individual receives $100 taxable income, i.e., an income of $100 in excess of the exemption and deductions, he pays tax. Under the proposal, if his taxable income is minus $100, i.e., $100 less than the exemption plus deductions, he would pay a negative tax, i.e., receive a subsidy. If the rate of subsidy were, say, 50 per cent, he would receive $50. If he had no income at all, and, for simplicity, no deductions, and the rate were constant, he would receive $300. He might receive more than this if he had deductions, for example, for medical expenses, so that his income less deductions, was negative even before subtracting the exemption. The rates of subsidy could, of course, be graduated just as the rates of tax above the exemption are. . . .

The advantages of this arrangement are clear. . . . It gives help in the form most useful to the individual, namely, cash. It is general and could be substituted for the host of special measures now in effect. It makes explicit the cost borne by society. It operates outside the market. Like any other measure to alleviate poverty, it reduces the incentives of those helped to help themselves, but it does not eliminate that incentive entirely, as a system of supplementing incomes up to some fixed minimum would. An extra dollar earned always means more money available for expenditures.

No doubt there would be problems of administration, but these seem to me a minor disadvantage, if they be a disadvantage at all. The system would fit directly into our current income tax system and could be administered along with it . . . . More important, if enacted as a substitute for the present grab-bag of measures directed at the same end, the total administrative burden would surely be reduced.

A few brief calculations suggest also that this proposal could be far less costly in money, let alone in the degree of governmental intervention involved, than our present collection of welfare measures. . . .

In 1961, government outlays amounted to something like $33 billion (federal, state, and local) on direct welfare payments and programs of all kinds: old age assistance, social security benefit payments, aid to dependent children, general assistance, farm price support programs, public housing, etc. I have excluded veterans' benefits in making this calculation. . . .

There are approximately 57 million consumer units (unattached individuals and families) in the United States [1962]. In 1961 expenditures of $33 billion would have financed outright cash grants of nearly $6,000 per consumer unit to the 10 per cent with the lowest incomes. . . . Even if one went so far as that one-third whom New Dealers were fond of calling ill-fed, ill-housed, and ill-clothed, 1961 expenditures would have financed grants of nearly $2,000 per consumer unit. . . .

The major disadvantage of the proposed negative income tax is its political implications. It establishes a system under which taxes are imposed on some to pay subsidies to others. And presumably, these others have a vote. There is always the danger that instead of being an arrangement under which the great majority tax themselves willingly to help an unfortunate minority, it will be converted into one under which a majority imposes taxes for its own benefit on an unwilling minority. . . . I see no solution to this problem except to rely on the self-restraint and good will of the electorate.

GUARANTEEING AN INCOME

Abridged from "Guaranteeing an Income" by Robert Theobald, from THE COMMONWEAL (September 4, 1964). Reprinted by permission of the author.

1 How does Theobald compare guaranteed income with limited liability for stockholders?
2 How does Theobald use the present income tax laws to justify his proposal?
3 How does Theobald's proposal differ from one that would change the present income tax laws to give more exemptions to persons with low incomes?

Every citizen of the United States and everybody who has resided in the United States for a period of five consecutive years should be guaranteed the right to an income sufficient to enable him to live with dignity. . . .

This right would apply equally to every member of society and should carry with it no connotation of personal inadequacy or implication that an undeserved income was being received from an overgenerous government. On the contrary, the implication would be one of responsibility by the total society for ensuring that no member of the society lived in a manner incompatible with the standards acceptable to his fellow men *merely because* he lacked purchasing power.

The guaranteed income plan can be compared to the introduction of limited liability in the nineteenth century. Limited liability was introduced in the nineteenth century to allow risk-taking by companies—the stockholder's liability no longer extended to his total wealth but only to the amount invested in the company. Limited liability was a pre-condition for the taking of risks: it did not ensure risk-taking or innovation but only made them possible.

Similarly, a guaranteed income provides the individual with the ability to do what he personally feels to be important; thus allowing risk-taking. It provides him with a minimum income which prevents his complete dependence on any other individual. . . .

The introduction of limited liability can be compared to the introduction of a guaranteed income for another reason. The proposal to introduce limited liability in the nineteenth century was deeply shocking: it justified failure to pay legitimate creditors. The proposal to introduce a guaranteed income is similarly shocking in the twentieth century—it justifies income without toil.

It is also interesting to note that the justifications for the two measures are similar. The reason limited liability was introduced in the nineteenth century was that it was essential if society was to achieve its goal of industrial growth. The reason why a guaranteed income must be introduced in the immediate future is because it is essential if we are to preserve our goal of individual freedom. . . .

What historical, social and philosophical justifications exist for a guaranteed income? We can turn to the ideas of Jefferson who believed that there could be no freedom without the possession of personal property, usually land, that without personal property each man and his family would be "slaves" of his employer and the currently accepted views of society. This remains a basic truth, that unless a man has independent means he can seldom afford to dissent.

During the early years of the American industrial revolution, the prospect of work for money wages attracted immigrants from abroad and workers off the subsistence farms. Later, as the productive potential of the economy increased, Henry Ford introduced the concept that the money wages of the worker should represent a fair share of the wealth of the Nation—that a reasonable work-contribution should be recompensed with a reasonable wage. In the decades following the introduction of this concept by Ford, the level of industrial wages grew steadily throughout the nation and it came to be believed that the continued development of the industrial system and the attainment of high levels of material prosperity would eventually provide a high standard of living for all.

At about the same time as Ford introduced the $5 day, the

federal government found its income inadequate to meet its obligations. The government, therefore, introduced a federal income tax system which was designed to obtain limited amounts of money from those citizens whose incomes were more than sufficient to enable them to maintain a reasonable standard of living.

Two basic principles were inherent in the United States tax system from its inception. First, that each person would only pay taxes when his income exceeded the level required to provide a decent standard of living. Second, that any income above this level would be subject to "progressive" taxation: that, the larger the total amount of income received, the greater would be the percentage paid in tax. This latter principle was, of course, meant to ensure that the rich would pay a larger percentage of their income in taxes than the poor.

During World War II, however, the implied contract between the government and the people, which stated that sufficient income to cover reasonable expenses would be tax free, was broken and the amount of income exempted from tax was reduced to $500. The Encyclopedia Britannica describes the effect of this step in the following way: "At the beginning of World War II, the tax was converted almost overnight from a 'rich man's tax' to one which reached down to the great majority of workers. . . . The number of returns, which had been 6,000,000 in 1937, touched 50,000,000 in 1945. . . ." As a result, for the first time, people whose incomes were below the level required for reasonable subsistence were obliged to pay federal income taxes.

The war and the emergency which justified taxing the poor are over. We can hardly rest content with a system which requires that the poor members of society contribute to the federal treasury, *and* to local and state treasuries, *even though their income is inadequate to meet even their minimum subsistence needs.* It is not generally known that a study by the Tax Foundation, of the tax burden in the year 1958 showed that the proportion of an individual's income paid in federal, state and local taxes does not vary significantly until the income of the individual rises above $15,000—in other words, an average individual earning less than $2,000 pays approximately as large a percentage of his income in taxes as an individual earning between $10,000 and $15,000.

127

Gabriel Kolko has shown in his book *Wealth and Power in America* that the taxes levied on the poorest class of society by the federal government are more than sufficient to pay for the total welfare benefits made available to them by the federal government. He states that in the year 1958, families and individuals earning less than $4,000 contributed over $6 billion to the federal treasury. "But the federal government spent only $4,509 million [$4.509 billion] on what by the most generous definition may be called 'welfare' . . . If all federal welfare expenditures went to the $0-$4,000 class—which was certainly not the case—this class more than paid for them." . . . Federal government benefits do not transfer money from the rich to the poor in any major amount—the main result of this federal activity is to transfer income from *some* poor people to *other* poor people.

The practical method of distributing the income due under the guaranteed income proposal would be to reactivate the original principles of the federal income tax system. We should reestablish the principle that the portion of income required to maintain a reasonable standard of living should be tax free. Taxes should only be paid on incomes rising above this level. Once this level has been established, those whose incomes from earnings and capital do not reach this level should be entitled to receive federal government payments sufficient to raise their incomes to this level and ensure their *basic economic security.*

At what levels should entitlements be set initially? Two factors must be taken into account in making this decision: first, the necessity of providing an income adequate for minimum subsistence for everybody; and, second, the necessity to prevent the overburdening of the administrative operation at the time payments are introduced. It might be expected that a level of $1,000 for every adult and $600 for every child would be feasible as a starting point for calculations. . . . Present incomes are so low for a substantial part of the population that a guaranteed income at these levels would benefit about *twenty million Americans* or one person in nine.

The United States can easily afford these levels of payment. The President's Council of Economic Advisers, in its 1964 annual report, calculated the cost of eliminating extreme poverty. They stated: "Conquest of poverty is well within our power. About $11 billion would bring all poor families up to the $3,000 income level we have taken to be the minimum for a decent life. . . . The burden —one-fifth of the annual defense budget, less than 2 percent of GNP —would certainly not be intolerable."

**THE COMING CRISIS
IN WELFARE**

"The Coming Crisis in Welfare" by Henry Hazlitt from NATIONAL REVIEW, (April 4, 1967). Reprinted by permission of National Review, 150 East 35th Street, New York, New York 10016.

1 Is Hazlitt's major criticism based on his convictions about human behavior or on the economic implications of the proposals?
2 Why does Hazlitt feel that the negative income tax plan is superior to the guaranteed income plan?
3 Does Hazlitt think that the government should be responsible for a person who needs economic assistance?
4 Does Hazlitt support existing relief and welfare measures? Why or why not?

The Negative Income Tax as proposed by Prof. Milton Friedman is essentially, with one modification, just one more form of the guaranteed annual income. . . .

In the words of Mr. Robert Theobald, one of its [guaranteed annual income] principal sponsors, this proposal "would guarantee to every citizen of the United States . . . the right to an income from the Federal Government to enable him to live with dignity." . . .

The recipients are to continue to get this guaranteed income, let me emphasize, not only if they resolutely refuse to seek or take a job, but if they throw the handout money away at the races, or spend it on prostitutes, or whisky, marijuana, or what not. . . .

The first thing to be said about this scheme economically is that if it were put into effect it would not only be intolerably expensive to the taxpayers who were forced to support it, but that it would destroy the incentives to work and to produce on an unparalleled scale. . . .

Who. . .would be willing to take the smelly jobs, or any low-paid job, once the guaranteed income program is in effect? . . .

Now suppose that you are a married man with two children, and your present income from some nasty and irregular work is $2,500 a year. The government would then send you a check for $500. But it would very soon occur to you that though you now had $3,000, you could have got this $3,000 without doing any work at all.

The scheme is not only economically but morally indefensible. If *"everybody* should receive a guaranteed income as a matter of right"* (the words just quoted are Mr. Theobald's), who is to pay him that income?

The truth is, of course, that the government has nothing to give to anybody that it doesn't first take from someone else. The whole guaranteed income proposal is a perfect modern example of the shrewd observation of the French economist Bastiat more than a century ago: "The state is the great fiction by which everybody tries to live at the expense of everybody else." . . .

The negative income tax (a misnomer for an income subsidy) suffers from most of the economic, political and moral vices of the guaranteed income. But it does have one important advantage over the guaranteed-income proposal in its cruder form: at least it would not destroy the incentive to work and produce to the same appalling extent.

Under the negative income tax, a man or a family would receive from the government a subsidy of 50 per cent, say, of the amount by which the family income fell below the so-called poverty-line income—let us say $3,000 a year. This means that if the family had no income at all it would receive a subsidy of $1,500. If it already had an earned income of $1,500, it would receive a government subsidy of $750, and so on.

Prof. Friedman, the distinguished author of this proposal, admits that, "like any other measures to alleviate poverty," his proposal would reduce "the incentives of those helped to help themselves"; but he goes on to argue, quite correctly, that it would not eliminate that incentive entirely, as the system of supplementing incomes up to some fixed minimum would. Under his plan an extra dollar earned would . . . mean more money . . . for expenditure. . . .

The negative income tax of Prof. Friedman, as put forward in 1962 in his book *Capitalism and Freedom,* was a . . . modest proposal. He suggested that if a man had no income at all, he would receive a basic subsidy of $300. Once this idea got into practical politics, however, this basic sum would soon be denounced as utterly inadequate to allow a family of four to live in "decency and dignity." In fact, the humanitarian reformers would soon be demanding a basic subsidy of $3,000 or $4,000 to a family otherwise without income, and we would be back to the same starting point as the guaranteed income scheme. . . .

Instead of a rigid ceiling, like the guaranteed income, the negative income tax would provide for a gradual tapering off. But otherwise it suffers from all the fatal flaws of the guaranteed-income proposal. Both would take money away from those who were earning it to turn it over both to those who could not earn it and those who refused to earn it. Money would be given to people whose incomes were low, without any regard to the reasons why those incomes were low. A person whose income was low or non-existent because he was a beatnik or a loafer or a drunk would get just as much, and no questions asked, as a person whose income was low or non-existent because he was blind or disabled or sick or the victim of some accident or circumstance beyond his control.

So far I have been summarizing arguments . . . against both the guaranteed income and the negative income tax. Prof. Friedman's reply to these . . . is peculiar. . . .

Friedman begins by telling his conservative and libertarian critics that they are foolish to object to the guaranteed income because we already "have a governmentally guaranteed income in substance though not in name." Even if his contention were true, it would be irrelevant to the merits of the case. If we already have a guaranteed income then the thing to do is to get rid of it.

Friedman then makes the undeniable statement that our present "grab-bag of relief and welfare measures" is "a mess." Precisely; and throwing the negative income tax on top of it would turn the mess into a nightmare.

But, Friedman insists, he is not proposing to throw his negative income tax on top of this mess; he is proposing to repeal all the existing relief and welfare measures and *substitute* his scheme for them.

Now who is living in a "dream world"? Does Friedman seriously believe that the veterans will quietly give up their pensions? That the farmers will calmly surrender their price supports and other subsidies? That the beneficiaries of subsidized public housing will cheerfully agree to pay a full economic rent? That we will soon hear the last of "free education" at the college level; of free school lunches; of food stamps? Will the workers give up unemployment compensation? Will the great mass of the voters give up any of their promised Social Security benefits? Will the elderly even give up the Medicare benefits they have just acquired? . . .

Speaking for myself, I am not opposed to the negative income tax merely because I regard it as a political certainty that it would be far bigger than Friedman proposes and would simply be thrown on top of the immense welfare burden (in the neighborhood of $50 billion a year) that the American taxpayers already carry. I am opposed to it in principle. It is far inferior to the traditional methods of relief. Generations of experience with relief plans show that they will quickly get out of control and be subject to gross abuse, fraud, and chiseling, unless a means test is retained, unless there is some case-by-case and applicant-by-applicant examination—in brief, unless the recipients of unearned income from the government are subject to at least as much checking and investigation as income-tax payers. . . .

We are confronted with a grave and immensely difficult problem, which we are bound to face candidly. Where any person, a child or an adult, is in fact helpless, or sick or disabled, or hungry, or jobless through no moral fault of his own, and where no private person or group is responsible for him, should "society," acting through government, make itself responsible?

The overwhelming majority of people would answer Yes. Since far back in history "society" has, in fact, assumed this responsibility. . . .

The problem is, granted this responsibility, how can the government mitigate the penalties of failure and misfortune without undermining the incentives to effort and success? How can it prevent the abuse of relief and the ominous growth of an ever-bigger army of relief recipients?

I suspect that there is no perfect solution to this problem, but at best a least unsatisfactory solution.

But of one thing we can be reasonably certain. As long as

those on relief have the vote while they remain on relief, politicians will continue to increase the burden of relief and welfare until it brings on hyper-inflation, insolvency, the wholesale destruction of incentives, or some other form of social and economic crisis. . . .

. . . [D]oes he [Friedman] himself believe that in the present political climate there is any possibility of his negative income tax being enacted in the modest form he proposes—and as a *substitute* for, instead of still another addition to, the present $50 billion worth of all other forms of relief and welfare now so solidly entrenched?

If he does believe that, he is really out on Cloud 9.

**THE PITFALLS
OF GUARANTEED INCOME**

Abridged from "The Pitfalls of Guaranteed Income" by Sar A. Levitan from THE REPORTER (May 18, 1967). Copyright © 1967 by The Reporter Magazine Company. Reprinted by permission of the author.

1 What are some of the disadvantages of a negative income tax that Levitan brings out?
2 What does Levitan propose as a substitute for a guaranteed income?
3 According to Levitan what effect might the guaranteed income plan have on: (a) people with income-producing assets and (b) unemployed or underemployed people?

The implementation of any guaranteed income plan, including the negative income tax, must resolve two basic issues: the amount of aid that would be given to the poor and the impact that the guaranteed income would have upon the incentive to work. In its simplest form, a negative income tax would allow the poor to claim a predetermined portion of their income below the poverty threshold. For example, according to government statistics, the poverty threshold for a family of four is about $3,130. Assuming that the negative income-tax rate were fixed at fifty per cent, a family of four with an annual income of $1,000 would receive an additional $1,065 from the government. If the family had no income at all, its total negative income tax would be $1,565, or fifty per cent of its total minimum needs. The net annual cost of such a plan, after deduction of current public-assistance payments, would amount to about $5 billion. It would alleviate poverty but would by no means eliminate it.

Other proposals for a negative income tax would eliminate poverty by overhauling the present tax system to grant poor people enough money to bring all of them up to the poverty threshold. For example, a family of four with an income of $2,000 a year would receive a grant of $1,130; if the family had no income, it would receive $3,130. Such a program would require payments totaling an estimated $11 billion a year. However, the guarantee of a poverty-level income would remove the pecuniary [financial] incentives for millions of people to work, since their incomes would remain at the poverty threshold whether or not they held jobs. Ten million workers in the United States earn less than $1.50 an hour—that is, $3,000 a year or less even if they work full time throughout the year. To counter this possibility of lessened incentive, a workable plan must permit low-wage earners to keep at least a portion of their earned income. Thus a family of four with an income of $3,000 might be able to claim a negative income tax of, say, $1,200, making its total income higher than the family without a wage earner. This would, of course, increase the cost of the program beyond the $11 billion needed simply to bring all poor people up to the poverty threshold. The magnitude of the cost would depend on the extent of incentives that any plan would provide. . . .

Aside from the high costs, a negative income tax would raise many new problems. It would distribute uniform minimum amounts to all beneficiaries. But the cost of living varies widely among urban areas and between urban and rural areas. . . .

A guaranteed income program also contains serious administrative difficulties and lends itself to abuse. Owners of small businesses, farmers, or persons with other income-producing assets could divest themselves of their income by deeding or gifting their properties, whereupon they would become entitled to receive the full measure of guaranteed income. While such abuses might be minimized by Internal Revenue Service detective work, the problem of determining eligibility would remain. . . . How would the income deficit of the negative income-tax recipient be paid? If he had to wait until his income deficit made him eligible, he would not receive the aid when he needed it most. On the other hand, if payments were made on the basis of income anticipations, they would be based on guesses; and if actual income exceeded advance estimates, the subsidies would have to be repaid—a difficult burden on low-income recipients. In addition, beneficiaries would not be able to predict illnesses or other unforeseen mishaps. Under these circumstances, a negative income tax would still have to be supplemented by some form of public assistance.

Another inherent deficiency of the negative income tax is that income differentials between skilled and unskilled workers would be reduced. . . . Would it discourage apprenticeship or the learning of skills? Would skilled workers succeed in pushing up differentials narrowed by the guaranteed income and thus increase inflationary pressures? . . .

The impact that the guaranteed income would have on participation of the labor force, or the willingness of people to work once they are assured a minimal income, is even more in doubt. It would depend partly upon the level of the guaranteed income. . . . Many of the poor are stranded in slums or in depressed areas and in impoverished rural areas where work opportunities are extremely limited. Even a modest guaranteed income might well become another barrier keeping many of these unemployed and underemployed workers from seeking gainful employment in areas where jobs are available. . . .

Since the poor are not a homogeneous lot, it should not come as a surprise that no single plan can be adapted to their needs. Social Security already provides a very effective vehicle to supply income to the aged. Unfortunately, the present minimum benefits are too low and leave many of the aged in dire poverty. President Johnson's proposal to raise the minimum from $44 to $70 per month would help to reduce poverty among the aged, and raising the minimum by another few dollars would practically eliminate it. This can be done with little concern that income guarantees for the five million aged poor would reduce incentives to work and, anyway, the present law permits recipients of Social Security to earn an additional $1,500 a year without reducing their benefits. [Note: social security rates were increased in 1968.]

To provide income for the other twenty-seven million poor,

a means test remains necessary, keeping in mind the observation of a perceptive social worker that "a means test does not have to be mean." . . .

The level of public-assistance benefits in most states should also be raised. At present, each state determines the annual cost of basic needs. The median basic needs calculated by the states for a mother with three children on AFDC [Aid to Families with Dependent Children] is about $2,500. However, in two of every three states the actual benefits fall below this predetermined minimum need. In a recent message to Congress, President Johnson proposed that each state be required to pay the full amount of basic needs according to its own determination. In addition, the President proposed that monthly earnings up to $150 per family would not affect the level of benefits that a family is entitled to receive under public assistance. A better plan for providing incentive to work would permit a family to maintain a predetermined proportion of any earned income, depending upon its need. Adoption of this type of proposal with a simplified means test would greatly improve the public-assistance program and would leave social workers free to help rehabilitate families and offer them necessary social services that would help them escape from poverty.

Finally, there will still be many employable members of families on public assistance. The best way to help them escape poverty is to provide them with employment opportunities. This can be achieved either through the government's assuming the responsibility as "an employer of last resort," providing jobs to potential workers who cannot secure employment on the open market, or by subsidizing private employers to provide jobs for the poor.

QUESTIONS FOR CLOSER STUDY

1 "Friedman's proposal is less radical and more realistic than Theobald's." Explain why you agree or disagree with the quotation.

2 Do you think that a negative income tax would lower the aspirations and goals of unskilled workers? Why or why not?

3 "The basic difference between Hazlitt and Theobald is their attitude toward man." Why do you agree or disagree?

4 Can it be said that Levitan's critique is less emotional and based on better evidence than Hazlitt's? Why or why not?

5 Which of Levitan's criticisms do you consider to be the most important? Why?

6 Do you think that responsibility for alleviation of poverty lies more with the federal government or with local government? Why?

7 How do you think the economy would be affected if billions of dollars were put into the hands of those with very low incomes?

CHAPTER 8

AUTOMATION:
BLESSING OR CURSE?

Automation is a production technique in which machines assume the menial and routine tasks of many workers. These machines, operated by only a few workers, can accomplish many clerical tasks as well as produce huge quantities of goods. The wholesale replacement of workers by machines has been terrifying to labor, but even more significant is the recent development whereby man's control and decision-making functions are being taken over by machines. This development in technology is called cybernetics.

People now accept technological change as inevitable, but it continues to be a threat to the security of many workers. The factory system, which grew out of the Industrial Revolution in eighteenth-century England, brought about dramatic changes in the life of the average man. Before the new industrial era, the average man was a farm worker or a cottage handicrafter. Gradually, he ceased to own the tools of production and became merely a cost unit in the owner's factory. His worth was determined by the factory owners, and his security was loosely governed by the law of supply and demand as it applied to labor.

Today automation occupies a central position in the conflict between management and labor. Management sees in automation and cybernation the possibilities of lower labor costs and more efficient production leading to greater profits. Labor sees loss of jobs and elimination of certain trades leading to loss of power. If, for example, a computer can be programmed to set type, highly skilled union linotype operators or typesetters become unnecessary to the printing industry. Despite differences, management and labor realize that technological change has raised the standard of living in many nations.

The lines of controversy, then, are clearly drawn; the arguments on either side seem equally valid depending on a person's point of reference or special area of interest. Furthermore, the increased power of labor in recent years has created a more even match in the dispute between labor and management over technological change.

The first reading, taken from a 1966 publication of the American Federation of Labor-Congress of Industrial Organizations (AFL-CIO), argues that unemployment and other human suffering resulting from automation are not necessary and that Americans should act to correct such trends.

The second reading is by economist Garth L. Mangum. Concerned with the impact of automation, Mangum maintains that unemployment is due more to fluctuating economic growth than to automation. He points out that, while technological change does lead to unemployment in certain fields, the general employment

138

level rises with economic expansion. Mangum's article, which appeared in the January 1966 *Labor Law Journal,* calls for retraining of displaced workers.

The third reading is by Robert B. Cooney, assistant editor of the *AFL-CIO American Federationist.* Published in May 1964, it describes the effects of technological change on highly skilled workers.

The last article is excerpted from a speech that Roger Blough, chairman of the board of directors of the United States Steel Corporation, delivered on January 21, 1964. Blough feels that technological change is inevitable, that its importance as a cause of unemployment is debatable, and that it should be treated as a challenge rather than as a curse.

THE PRICE OF TECHNOLOGICAL PROGRESS

Abridged from LABOR LOOKS AT AUTOMATION, (December 1966). Reprinted by permission of American Federation of Labor and Congress of Industrial Organizations.

1 Which kinds of occupations are most likely to be affected by automation?
2 Why is the Negro one of the first victims of automation?
3 How specific and helpful are labor's suggested solutions to the problems of automation?

The Push-Button Miner is a mechanical giant standing three stories high and weighing more than 1½ million pounds. It cuts and loads as much as 266 tons of coal an hour in one continuous operation, without drilling or blasting and with very little human intervention. The entire operation requires . . . only three men and is performed by remote control from a panel outside of the mine shaft.

Within the postwar period, machines similar to the Push-Button Miner have almost tripled the amount of coal which a man can mine in one day. They have made the American coal industry the most efficient in the world—. . . it can deliver coal to Europe more cheaply than Europeans can produce it, pay American miners far more than European miners, and still make a healthy profit.

These mechanical marvels, unfortunately, have also left a

trail of misery in their wake. Thousands of idled miners, trapped in one-industry coal towns, have been compelled to work in "dog-hole" mines at a fraction of their former wages. Others have fallen back temporarily upon unemployment benefits, exhausted their savings and ended up on relief. Long after the end of the 1960-61 recession, as much as 75 percent of the population of some coal mining areas subsisted on food and clothing distributed by the government.

In 1966, coal mining employment was about 75 percent below what it had been in 1948 and the names of coal mining communities —Harrisburg, Herrin and West Frankfort in Illinois; Corbin, Harlan, Hazard and Middlesboro in Kentucky; Scranton, Wilkes-Barre, Hazelton, Uniontown and Connellsville in Pennsylvania; and Beckley and Bluefield, in West Virginia—still dominated the list of areas of substantial unemployment despite more than five years of steady economic expansion in the nation as a whole.

Like the American coal industry, American agriculture is the most efficient in the world. Fertilizers, chemical weed killers, insecticides and new machines have almost tripled farm output per hour since 1947. Mechanical cotton pickers are now harvesting more than 90 percent of Mississippi's cotton crop and doing it more cheaply than men paid as little as $6 a day.

Like the coal industry, also, the new agricultural technology is a mixed blessing. Millions of small farm owners, sharecroppers, tenant farmers and regular hired hands have been uprooted. Some have become migratory workers and many others have drifted to the cities in search of a job.

For Negroes the exodus from the farm has posed very special difficulties. Thousands of displaced Negro sharecroppers and farm laborers have been left penniless and hungry with little to look forward to except the prospect of moving to a big city slum. "With technological progress far more to blame than racial prejudice," Newsweek reported in 1966, "up to 20,000 Delta Negro farm laborers are expected to be idle this cotton season—a staggering total that amounts to half the shrunken pool of workers still working the blackbelt soil of Mississippi." And soon many of the remaining 1½ million Negroes now living on southern and border state farms will be faced with the same problem.

One-industry coal towns and one-crop farming communities are not the only places in which rapid technological change has left a trail of hardship. The Bureau of Labor Statistics of the U.S. Department of Labor studied the effects of five mass layoffs "related in part to technological change . . . in substantially industrialized and highly diversified areas." The studies, made between April 1962 and April 1963, covered a petroleum refinery, an auto parts plant, a glass jar plant, a floor covering plant and two iron foundries. This is what they found:

Almost 25 percent of the 3000 workers who had been displaced were unemployed at the time the surveys were made—some six to 21 months after the five mass layoffs occurred. In one case, 39 percent of the displaced workers were still jobless.

In four out of the five cases studied, more than 40 percent of the displaced workers had been unemployed for a half-year or more.

In addition to those counted as unemployed, a significant number became "labor force dropouts." They stopped looking for jobs not because they did not want to work but because of their inability to find work.

More than half of those who were reemployed suffered a decline in earnings. The decline amounted to at least 20 percent for one out of every four reemployed workers.

More than half of the displaced workers had over 10 years of service and, in one plant, seven out of eight had at least 26 years of service. Most of these lost all of their seniority and all that it meant in terms of protection against layoffs, longer vacations, pension rights and other fringe benefits.

Is this the price which America must pay for technological progress? Must the American miner be plunged into a state of hopelessness in order to make mining more competitive? Must the Negro farm worker be driven to desperation in order to produce cotton more efficiently? To enable business to cash in on the potential savings of automation, must the factory worker suffer long layoffs, involuntary retirement, the loss of hard-earned benefits and a lower standard of living, even when he is lucky enough to find another job?

American labor believes that technological progress does not require such human sacrifices. The enormous productive power of the new technology need not be the cause of hardship and suffering. It can, instead, make life far better than most would have dared to hope just a few decades ago.

However, to transform the abundance which automation

now makes possible into a genuine blessing for all, America needs understanding, compassion and a sense of urgency.

It needs to understand how automation and other changes are revolutionizing American life; how these changes can contribute to massive unemployment; and how they can result in severe hardship for some people and communities even in the absence of massive unemployment.

It needs compassion to develop programs and to adjust the speed of technological change, when necessary, to avoid dumping masses of workers, polluting the environment, and otherwise hurting human beings.

And it needs to match its understanding and its compassion with a sense of the urgency of providing good jobs, adequate incomes and decent living conditions for all Americans. These goals have never been automatically achieved in the past and they are even less likely to be automatically achieved in the more highly automated society of the present or future. Only a carefully planned war on joblessness, want and social decay, on a massive scale, can make them a reality. And only a sense of urgency can mobilize sufficient resources to bring such a war to a quick and successful conclusion.

**CYBERNATION
AND JOB SECURITY**

Abridged from "Cybernation and Job Security" by Garth L. Mangum from LABOR LAW JOURNAL (January 1966). Reprinted by permission of the author, Commerce Clearing House, Inc. and Association of Labor Mediation Agencies.

1 What point is the author trying to make by giving examples of worker displacement by machines in 1929?
2 What evidence does he give to support his view that economic expansion causes high employment levels?
3 What is his solution to the problem of displacement of workers due to lack of education and skill?

To anyone exposed to the popular press over the past few years, the topic of cybernation and job security conjures up opposing visions. The factory without people—the full unemployment world—a monster called cybernation devouring jobs at the rate of two million a year—a world where a few scientists and engineers work short hours at high pay obsequiously obeying the commands of the computer. A handful of overworked professionals bear the major burdens of society while the masses, unemployed and unemployable, are provided with income and hobby-type activities as a substitute for a meaningful role in the world.

Less often, but just as reasonably, the vision is of the Golden Age—the abundant society, leisure well used, education and culture —the Agora and the Parthenon but with electronic slaves. But fortunately in one case and unfortunately in the other, both have little relation to reality, nor will they have in the near future. The prospects and problems discussed here are much more mundane. Practically, cybernation must be abandoned at the beginning and sights lowered and broadened to the impact of technological change. . . .

Concern for the economic and social consequences of technological change has been periodic but the circumstances were always the same—persistent unemployment and a search for an explanation. Note, for instance, the contemporary sound of the following examples [from 1929]: . . .

"(1) *Yardmen:* The switching yard of the *XYZ* Railroad at *N* employed 305 men. Partly as an experiment in increasing speed and efficiency, partly to meet a local problem of smoke and noise nuisance within a growing municipality, the *XYZ* electrified its switching yard. As a result, 151 men were able to do the work formerly requiring 305. Also, it was found that less skill and experience on the part of the switching yard force was called for under the new conditions. Accordingly, 154 men were laid off on a week's notice.

"(2) *Glassworkers:* The Owens machine, which mechanized the ancient glassblowing industry, is a "semi-automatic" machine. More recently, it has been supplemented by a feed-and-flow machine, which makes several divisions of the glass industry practically automatic. It has been estimated that this machine does in 1 hour what it would take 41 workers to do by hand, and with it, 3 operatives can accomplish what 10 could do with the semi-automatic equipment. . . .

"(3) *Steelworkers:* The use of machinery and power has advanced rapidly throughout the steel industry in the past few years. For example, 2 men now do the work done by 14 in charging furnaces; 7 men can cast as much pig iron as 60 could cast a decade ago; in the open-hearth operation, 1 man does the work of 40; 2 men now replace 128 in unloading pig iron. . . .

"(4) *Musicians:* The Rialto Theater in a large eastern city has an orchestra of 40 trained musicians. The Rialto installed a "talking movie," and overnight these 40 musicians were out of a job.". . . The direct relationship between a particular machine installed and particular workers displaced has always been obvious. The complex relationships between all of the factors effecting economic growth and a high general level of unemployment are not directly observable. Throughout the immediate postwar period, unemployment averaged a comfortable 3 per cent of the labor force. But following the Korean War, unemployment levels drifted persistently upward over succeeding business cycles until between 1954 and 1964 it averaged 5.4 per cent.

In search for an explanation a debate arose, only the vague outlines of which are necessary to this discussion. The two schools of thought were the "expansionists" who were convinced the problem was simply a deficiency of aggregate demand resulting in a retarded economic growth rate, and the structuralists who looked for an explanation in the concentration of unemployment among the unskilled, the uneducated, the old, the young and the nonwhite. Paradoxically, there were some within each group who attributed a major role to technology. The more extreme of the expansionists were convinced that our technology had become so productive and our private wants so near satiation that a rate of economic growth compatible with full employment was unlikely. For some the answer was public expenditures and public employment; for others acceptance of unemployment and the guaranteed annual income. On the other hand, the assumption was general among structuralists that technological change had raised education and skill requirements beyond existing levels of attainment and had drastically increased the rate at which workers were being displaced by machines. By examining these four premises we can gain considerable insight into the lack of job security . . . .

Looking backwards from a period when renewed growth has begun to reduce unemployment, analysis is not too difficult. The economy simply did not grow fast enough. The key to understanding the general level of unemployment is the relationship among economic growth, productivity increase and labor force growth. So long as economic growth exceeds the increase in labor productivity, employment must rise. Unless the GNP rises more rapidly than the sum of productivity increase and labor force growth, unemployment will increase. The former was true in all but two of the post-Korean War years. The latter occurred in 6 out of 12 of the same years. . . .

Unemployment has been structural. It has been concentrated by age, sex, race, skill, education and geographical area. But it has always had a structure and that structure, except for the present dramatic increase in the youth component, has not worsened. Even youth are the best educated group ever to enter any labor force. There are just so many of them.

It is useful to conceive of the labor force as a gigantic 75 million man shape-up. The workers queue up in order of their relative attractiveness to employers. The employers go down the line one by one until they have filled their manpower needs. The leftovers will always be the most disadvantaged but how far the employer reaches down the queue depends primarily upon the demand for his products. Improving the quality of those at the foot of the line improves their ability to compete but only in a limited sense increases the number of jobs. . . .

Technological change has had little to do with the high general rates of unemployment which have interfered with job security and made collective bargaining difficult over the past few years. Not that technological change has not caused displacement of workers. It has, but it has been only one of many changing forces. The rate of displacement for technological and other reasons affects the level of frictional unemployment. How difficult it is for the displaced worker to find new employment is determined by the aggregate level of economic activity. The costs—human, public and inflationary —of reducing unemployment can be lessened by a simultaneous aggregative and structural attack . . . .

Are the necessary growth rates conceivable? The growth requirement is also the growth potential. We have the manpower; we have the technology; we have the needs. Satiation of demand cannot be taken seriously in a nation with one-fifth in poverty, 6.3 per cent with incomes above $15,000 per year and only 1.2 per cent with incomes above $25,000 and facing a 35-year backlog of unmet public needs. The creation of purchasing power is economically a relatively simple task. The only necessities are the decision to act and the choice between tax reduction with allocation of resources to private production or public expenditure increases and attack on social problems. . . .

Under the best of conditions, workers in an industrial society will face insecurity. We have never been willing to provide for industrial workers the protections we consider standard for managers and professionals. The more dynamic the economy the greater the changes in manpower requirement will be, but the greater the new job opportunities will be as well. The goal of public manpower policy is to reduce the pain of change without losing its advantages. A threat to job security need not be a threat to worker security. The necessary though not sufficient insurance of the latter is a total commitment to full employment. Given that, assistance in retraining, relocation and placement can ease the transition from one job to another. At the same time collective bargaining can help compensate for the substantial losses in accumulated job rights incident to job change.

Change is never without hardship but its costs can be reduced. There can be no job security without an adequate rate of job creation. The state of economic knowledge is such that a satisfactory rate of job creation is a matter of public policy choice.

**AUTOMATION: THE IMPACT
ON JOBS AND PEOPLE**

Abridged from ''Automation: The Impact on Jobs and People'' by Robert B. Cooney from *AFL-CIO American Federationist*, (May 1964). Reprinted by permission of American Federation of Labor and Congress of Industrial Organizations.

1 What effects does the author think computers will have on the level of education among workers?
2 Why will routine ''blue-collar'' workers be hardest hit by automation?
3 What specific proposals have labor and management made to ease the impact of automation?
4 In what ways may automation help the worker?

The leading edge of radical technological change is now slicing its way through America's offices, factories and stores, undercutting familiar ways of working and living. As the changes intensify, there may follow social and political repercussions unless imaginative programs are devised to help people adjust to new roles.

The computer—the symbol of the radical change—is inspiring a revolution of attitude and practice which will hurt first those least able to adjust: the less skilled, the less educated, the Negro and other minority groups, the people moving from rural to urban areas. These dispossessed will be joined in the years ahead by those who now feel secure in a skill, for if a job involves routine then a computer-guided machine can do it better and faster.

This is the pace of change: workers automated off their assembly line are now being retrained as draftsmen at the same time a company has marketed a low-priced tape-controlled, computer-fed automatic drafting machine. Before they have learned a second skill, it is already potentially obsolete.

A national computer congress held in Washington, D.C., in mid-April [1964] attracted some 5000 computer professionals and unveiled the latest in computers. A prominent expert warned that computers and automation are moving in on skilled technicians and middle management. He said all "routine, uncreative" jobs can be programmed through and performed by computers. Beyond this, exhibitors showed that computers can handle routine creative jobs like producing animated movies, designing bridges and buildings and performing medical diagnoses once done by the family doctor.

. . . But the technological change underway involves many things: greater mechanization; new processes, materials, techniques and markets; reorganized plants; changed workforce skills and so on. In short, increased productivity—more output per manhour.

If these changes ripple rapidly enough through the nation's workplaces, the "moderately faster" rate of productivity foreseen for the remainder of the 1960s could climb more sharply. The result would be higher unemployment unless production and sales at least keep pace. . . .

And it is mainly unemployment which underlies and aggravates the nation's troubles, be it civil rights demonstrations, . . . rising welfare costs or juvenile delinquency. Decent jobs at good pay are desperately needed if these problems are to be resolved. If the pace of automation quickens, these problems can worsen.

Rapid economic growth is the key to the nation's problems, in the view of . . . national leaders. The economic growth rate must be high enough to create jobs for the 1.3 million new job-seekers entering the labor force each year, to dent unemployment and to provide job openings for those displaced by . . . technology. . . .

Looking back, America has seen technology bring miracles of production in agriculture which are the envy of other nations— but which forced millions out of farming and left them ill-prepared for city life. The nation has seen technological advances which have made the American coalminer the world's most productive—and left many miners and their families and their region in poverty. The nation has seen a pioneering textile industry turned into a decaying shell by migrating management. And it has seen meat-packing decentralize out of Chicago, once famous as "hog butcher to the world," leaving thousands jobless. . . .

An authoritative survey of informed people in the computer field has produced these findings:

Impact on jobs. Automated equipment is seen to have a very pronounced capacity to cut labor needs, even though it may be purchased to reduce waste and increase accuracy. . . .

Applying automation. Barriers to automation are rapidly being reduced. The shortage of personnel trained to understand the capabilities of automation is disappearing. . . .

Computer centers and less costly equipment also are making the new technology available to smaller businesses, thus tapping a new market. . . .

Research. Spending for research and development has been shooting upward—from $5 billion annually in 1953-54 to $10 billion a year in 1957-58 to $16 billion annually in 1962-63. Though much of this is for the military, out of it has come such advances as tape-controlled machine tools, molecular electronics, etc. The research of the 1950s is now bearing fruit.

These developments set the stage for radical changes in the economy. The best-informed people in the field, assuming the steady spread of automation, speculate that productivity could rise "at a still more rapid rate" in the 1970s and make the need even more urgent for bold programs.

But the overall productivity rate is similar to the case of the man who drowned trying to walk across a stream with an average depth of three feet. As experts warn, the overall rate conceals critical changes within industries. They note that non-farm productivity rose by 21 percent from 1950 to 1960. But, in soft coal, productivity shot up by 51.6 percent in the same decade while output slipped only 5.6 percent. The result: mining jobs plummeted by 440,000 or 36 percent.

Thus the point is made by experts that, even on assumptions that total national output will go up by 50 percent from 1960-70 and unemployment will be lowered to 3 percent, automation will lead the way to jobs cuts in many industries. . . .

In terms of the broad impact of automation on skills and people, experts see it this way. Automation does not require much higher skills from workers, who often can be trained to operate such equipment. But as such equipment becomes more sophisticated, it will thin out the ranks of even the more skilled employees. As automation devours routine blue-collar jobs, these workers will be thrown into the intensified competition for generally lower-paying jobs in the white-collar and service fields. As automation eats its way up the skill ladder, the job-changing it causes will be a matter of survival of the best-educated and best-skilled. . . .

To ease the impact of technological change, labor and management have devised a variety of methods of adjustment.

Collective bargaining agreements usually call for advance notice of a layoff or shutdown, but often this is no longer than a week. Automation is inspiring provisions requiring several months' notice.

Other approaches include the avoidance of layoffs through attrition, early retirement, work-spreading, retraining, transfer and relocation.

Cushioning actual layoffs are such devices as severance pay, vesting of pension rights, aid in retraining and placement elsewhere, supplemental jobless benefits. . . .

The urgent need, they stress, is for vigorous private and public employment policies to help equip workers with the education, skill and mobility needed to meet the fastchanging patterns of work and opportunity.

The new technology can help end monotonous, deadening

and dangerous work; it can help end want. It can also destroy. It will take man's best efforts to tame and control technology for the benefit of all. But there must be rapid economic growth to provide jobs and a favorable setting.

**THE ART
OF BEING SECURE**

From "The Art of Being Secure" by Roger M. Blough, from VITAL SPEECHES, (February 15, 1964). Reprinted by permission of City News Publishing Co.

1 Why is the article entitled "The Art of Being Secure"?
2 What factor, other than automation, does Blough feel must be taken into account in considering technological unemployment?
3 In what ways does the author feel that adjusting to change can solve the problems of unemployment due to automation?
4 What is his major argument against work-spreading devices?

The problem of unemployment persists in spite of the numerous and varied prescriptions that have been tried. The word "automation" is blazoned in the headlines and produces endless dialogue—reasoned or emotional. . . .

. . . There is no doubt that automation causes displacement of workers at one point and affords new job opportunities at another point; but there is no agreement as to whether the net effect is an increase or a decrease in overall employment and job security.

Yet in concentrating our attention, as we have, on automation, are we not forgetting the fact that this is only one facet of the great technological changes that are affecting job security—and a relatively small facet at that? Do we recognize that it is, perhaps, only the symptom of change, and not the major change itself?

We are concerned by what is happening to our established positions in the arrangement of things, and we are alarmed because the job that was, is no more. But do we also realize that in many cases, the product that was, and the company that was, are no more, either?

I suppose that no one enjoyed a greater measure of job security in his day than the healthy artisan who so ably performed his special work. Like the blacksmith—for example. So far as I know, no one ever produced a machine which made a better horseshoe, or could fit it, at lower-cost, to Dobbin's hoof. So the blacksmith's job security was not destroyed by automation. It simply disappeared as the horseshoe was replaced by the pneumatic tire.

I suppose, also, that being a member of a group—especially a large and successful group—adds greatly to a feeling of security in our job; but again, it is no guarantee. For group security also changes.

Of the hundred largest industrial corporations in 1909, only twenty-nine are still among the top hundred today. Of the other 71, some have disappeared, some have merged with more successful companies, and others have simply shrunk in relative position as newer, job-creating enterprises came into being.

Fifty years ago, for example, the three prestige automobiles in the country were the Pierce Arrow, the Peerless and the Packard; but they have gone with the wind of change. In recent years the Hudson, Nash and DeSoto, along with new entries like the Kaiser and Frazer cars, and the quarter-billion-dollar Edsel have fallen by the wayside. And so—of the 2700 different domestic automobile name plates that have been registered in the United States since 1893, fewer than 30 remain. The others? Time passed them by, and buried them in the dust of competition.

Today, under the merciless lash of competition, technological change is progressing at a furious—but, I feel, a still inadequate —pace. It is not only rendering old products, services and processes obsolete, but it is creating whole new industries so rapidly that the development of required skills within our workforce just does not seem to keep abreast of the changes.

Not long ago, *Reader's Digest* reprinted an advertisement which was originally published, deadpan, in *The Mines Magazine*. The ad read: "Wanted: Man to work on nuclear fissionable isotope molecular reactive counters and three-phase cyclotronic uranium photosynthesizers. No experience necessary."

And there is as much truth as humor in that, too. For how do you find experienced men in a field that never existed before? Yet these new fields are opening up every day, with new products and new processes that will again be obsolete tomorrow. . . .

Everywhere we turn, there is the fierce competition that is born of change; and the company which fails to meet that competition and to anticipate that change successfully will provide no job security for anyone. So our problem, it seems to me, is the whole field of change—and the intensified competition it is creating. And only as we comprehend the broad scope of its true dimensions can we hope to deal with that problem effectively.

Now change, of course, has been with us since the world began; and the world has not only survived it, but appears to have thrived upon it. What concerns us, then, is not so much change itself or the surging rapidity with which it is occurring, but how well we can adjust ourselves to change. So today—as has been true through the ages—we find people who would try to stop change, or retard it by throwing all kinds of economic obstacles in its path. . . .

Only by keeping abreast of change, I believe, can any nation maintain its security in this competitive world; and only by leading the race toward change can it increase its security and the well-being of all its people. Just keeping up will only perpetuate the problem. To solve it we must forge ahead.

So we are confronted by an interesting paradox: the more rapid and extensive the change, the greater the threat to individual job security there may seem to be, but the slower and more limited the change, the greater the threat to our collective security and our well-being as a people there undoubtedly will be.

The fear of change—this nostalgic clinging to things as they are—is understandable and a psychological characteristic, perhaps, of human nature. But let us remember that the kind of change we are discussing does not occur overnight, nor all at once. Studies indicate that from the time a technological innovation is proven in the laboratory to the time it comes into widespread commercial use, covers a span of ten to fifteen years as a rule; and that from the conception of the idea to the stage of widespread commercial use may well take fifty years. For example, the concept of the continuous casting of steel is at least a century old and Sir Henry Bessemer was one of the first to see its merits, but only in recent years has it been developed to the point of widespread feasibility.

So we do have time and opportunity to foresee major technological changes as they develop, and to plan for them and cope with them in an orderly way. How then do we do it?

More specifically, how do we care for those whose skills are no longer needed, and how—on the other hand—do we develop the new, and heretofore nonexistent, skills that technological change demands? How do we adjust our thinking and our training to solve the great paradox I have mentioned?

One vigorously-advocated proposal is that we institute a four-day week at five-days' pay, and then, presumably, progress—as necessary—to a three-day or a two-day week to spread the work. But this, of course, creates no new skills. It merely perpetuates the cultivation of old skills for which the need is disappearing. And even as a stop-gap measure, it is economically self-defeating. How can we hope to increase job security by adding to our costs when our competitive survival depends so heavily on the ability to reduce costs? Are we not jeopardizing the jobs of the many merely to give the illusion of greater job security for the few?

Another widely-advanced proposal is that a vast program of public works should provide jobs for those whose skills are no longer needed in industry. The theory here seems to be that once a man has held a job, he has some kind of vested right in it; and that if the progress of technological change makes that job obsolete, it becomes the responsibility of the employer, or of the group, or of society as a whole to support him thereafter—either in idleness or by providing him with unnecessary work that is suited to his skills.

The trouble with this proposal is, of course, that ultimately the number of persons to be supported will exceed the number who are able to provide the support, and job security will thus evaporate leaving a Sahara of poverty for all. . . .

It is said that today's skills will not hold tomorrow's jobs; and we must recognize that as true in a remarkably high percentage of cases.

We must recognize that the world does not owe us a living—in fact, that the world cannot afford to owe us a living even if it wanted to do so. Only we ourselves can provide that living. . . .

To sum it all up, then, it is undoubtedly true that many old products, old enterprises, old methods, and old jobs will disappear in the years ahead; and that many new products, enterprises, methods and jobs will replace them.

The degree of security that we shall possess as individuals, as groups, or as a nation will depend upon the willingness of each of us to prepare ourselves to meet these changes—to improve our own internal security. The opportunity will be there. We have only to help ourselves to it. But we shall never cultivate the art of being secure—internally or externally—by expecting others to do for us what we should and must do for ourselves. Nor will we—let me repeat—cultivate security as a people and as a nation by opposing the changes which, paradoxically, seems to threaten our security as individuals.

QUESTIONS FOR CLOSER STUDY

1 Would it be wise for labor to stand in the way of automation? Is it possible that management might suffer, in the long run, from too much automation? How?

2 Which writers seem to have the most specific and practical solutions to the problem of unemployment caused by automation?

3 In what ways, if any, is labor in a position to take action to reduce the effects of automation?

4 Do you agree with the conclusion that the answer to unemployment due to automation is economic growth? Why or why not?

5 Is it ever possible to have total job security? Why or why not?

CHAPTER 9

CAN WE MAKE THE
BUSINESS CYCLE
OBSOLETE?

One of the prevailing beliefs about the capitalist system is that business cycles—recurring periods of "boom and bust"—are inevitable. The economic history of the United States prior to World War II seemed to bear this out.

Since the Great Depression of the 1930's, however, the federal government has become increasingly active in attempting to protect the nation from the calamities of mass unemployment and business failures. "Stabilizers" such as tax cuts, farm-price supports, bank deposit insurance, public works programs, controls over interest rates and credit, and a social security program of old age pensions and unemployment insurance have been provided to guard against another severe economic downturn.

Because of these stabilizers some economists believe that the nation is immune to a prolonged depression like the one that followed the stock market collapse of 1929. Other economists feel that government intervention in economic affairs does not insure against depression and that the mechanics of the business cycle still operate. Still others believe that government intervention actually contributes to business instability and might ultimately lead to depression. There is at least some uneasiness whenever the nation's economy is in a period of rapid expansion. It is understandable that economists wonder if, as in the "boom" of the 1920's, the nation is also headed toward another "bust."

The four readings in this chapter bring out the opinions both of those economists who are convinced that the economy is safe from depression and those who are equally convinced that another depression is possible. The basic disagreement among them is not on whether the business cycle is or is not obsolete. Rather, it is on what can or cannot be done to make it obsolete.

The first reading is from an article written in 1954 by William H. Peterson, a United States Steel Corporation economist. Peterson believes that government interference in the economy greatly increases the chances of depression.

The second reading comes from an interview with economist Paul Samuelson in 1964. Samuelson is confident that because of the many built-in stabilizers and, more important, because of government determination to use them, depressions could be a thing of the past.

The third reading is from a 1965 speech by William McChesney Martin, Jr., Chairman of the Board of Governors of the Federal Reserve System. Noting parallels between the prosperity of the 1960's and that of the 1920's, Martin cautions against either complacency or recklessness.

The last reading is from a 1965 article by economist Robinson Newcomb. Newcomb says that serious business dips have been halted and claims that in a powerful, diversifying economy, even mild downswings, or recessions, are obsolete.

OUR ECONOMIC MAGINOT LINE

Abridged from "Our Economic Maginot Line" by Dr. William H. Peterson, from THE FREEMAN (June 14, 1954). Reprinted by permission of The Foundation for Economic Education, Inc.

1 Do you think Peterson's comparison of built-in economic stabilizers with the French Maginot line is valid? Why or why not?
2 Do you agree or disagree with the author's basic argument that economic stabilizers are paid for by taking money from those who have it and giving it to those who don't? Why?
3 Do you agree with Peterson that "extremes of boom and bust can be avoided if the government ceases its intervention into the economy"? Why or why not?

A growing opinion in Washington, New York, and points academic holds [that] an economic millennium has been reached. Never again another 1929. . . . Our "built-in" stabilizers will prevent the current dip from worsening beyond a recession. . . .

In France during the 1930's the politicians and the military had a similar sedative for national jitters. Never again another 1914 when the Huns lunged across the French border. The Maginot Line—the steel and concrete wall between France and Germany—was "impregnable."

In 1940 France fell in eighteen days.

Are we in for like disillusionment with our "economic defenses" against depression? It is maintained the economic stabilizers produce, among other things, a more constructive national psychology—a feeling of security against economic fluctuations, a tendency to spend more and save less, a faith that government devices will ward off economic shock. Dwight Eisenhower has said: "Never again shall we allow a depression in the United States." In 1928 Herbert Hoover suggested we were in sight of the day when poverty would be banished from America. Another Republican proclaimed: "We have reached a plateau of permanent prosperity."

Then came 1929.

The student of economic history takes issue with the claim that our economy is now "depression-proof." Professor James Washington Bell of Northwestern University recalls his being chided by his friends for continuing to give courses on Business Cycles during the latter twenties. "Don't you know that we have learned to lick business cycles?" they told him.

The American people are being given substantially the same line. In a recent handsome pamphlet, "Defense against Recession," the Committee for Economic Development says "our economy can achieve its high potential without violent fluctuations". . . .

The cycle of peak and trough, prosperity and depression has been checked, it must be admitted, but never denied. Government "contracyclical" action has prolonged depressions, as in the thirties when business confidence was shaken by government experimentation. It has also extended prosperity into a boom, as in the late twenties when the Federal Reserve depressed the interest rate in the 1926-29 period and thereby contributed to inflation, overinvestment, and speculation. Now the economic stabilizers of today: do they work and, if so, how well?

1. The farm price support program. Through this government intervention, described as a "formidable weapon" against depression by President Eisenhower in his Economic Report for 1954, farmers have a practically guaranteed income called "parity." But propping the income of farmers is in no sense a guarantee or even a contribution to *national* spending. The added income of farmers is taken from consumers in the form of higher grocery bills and taxes and "redistributed" to farmers. The farmers' gain is the consumers' loss. . . .

2. The unemployment compensation system. This system, backed by a trust fund of $9 billion, provides payments up to twenty-six weeks to the unemployed. "This helps to maintain sales," says an economic journal for businessmen. But here again is no magical manufacture of purchasing power. The employed carry the unemployed. . . .

3. The social security program. Spokesmen for this economic stabilizer say it aids in maintaining national spending "regardless of economic conditions." It is true that spending by the aged is sustained by payments out of the Old Age and Survivors Fund to

beneficiaries. But is *national* spending sustained if the group under sixty-five has its income reduced by social security taxes and by higher prices from employers' "contributions"? The young carry the old. . . .

4. Tax reduction. Also mentioned by the President as a "formidable weapon" to fight off depression is tax reduction. Apparently the theory of tax reduction is that in times of falling purchasing power the government can reduce taxes and thereby restore consumer purchasing power. . . . Ignored in the theory, however, is the lack of the sought-after effect of more purchasing power. Tax reduction is merely a transfer of purchasing power. The purchasing power restored to the taxpayers is exactly offset by the purchasing power taken from government spending agencies. . . .

5. The presence of strong labor unions. The rationale accorded this economic stabilizer argues that unions stabilize wage rates and sustain purchasing power during declines by resisting wage cuts or even increasing wage rates. But high wage rates, unless offset by higher productivity, involve high labor costs which are reflected in high rigid market prices. In effect, this means the unorganized consumer must pay higher prices for the benefit of the organized worker. The over-all effect on national purchasing power is nil. . . .

6. Public works. The President's Economic Report stresses public construction as a deterrent to depression. . . . [T]o pay for public works the government must tax or borrow. Either of these alternatives reduces private purchasing power, which could have similarly soaked up unemployment. When, as is likely the case, the government borrows at the Federal Reserve, the result is another dose of inflation. Public works, moreover, are located not so much as to need but as to politics. Many public works involve open competition with private enterprise—*e.g.*, hydro-electric facilities. . . .

7. Credit controls. . . . Advocates of this stabilizer hold that by making money "cheap" the wheels of production will be speeded up when the market slows down. The record of this theory in practice is unsatisfactory. When it "works" it creates over-borrowing, speculation, and a disturbance of the cost-price relationship, as in the late twenties. It does not "work" when either businessmen have already borrowed up to the hilt or they are pessimistic about the

outlook for profits. Cheap money policies flood the country with weakened dollars and tend to destroy the confidence of creditors and investors. . . .

8. Bank deposit insurance. This economic stabilizer operates under the theory that banking panics can be prevented by the preclusion of runs on banks. To an extent this is true, although the theory confuses cause with effect. The cause of bank failures is only partially explained by runs. It reaches into unsound loan portfolios and an over-invested business situation (largely resulting from government credit manipulation), which in turn prevent the banks from making good to their depositors. Federal insurance of bank deposits is not insurance at all, for the risk is not subject to natural phenomena and cannot be actuarially determined. It is rather the socialization of bank insolvencies, and has yet to face the critical test of a depression. . . .

Advocates of the foregoing devices optimistically view other factors which would supposedly see us through the threat of depression. Our growing population, for example, is touted as a guarantee of high consumer spending. "But population growth," as Lewis H. Haney pointed out in his syndicated column, "doesn't bring proportionate increase in production in China and India." The population enthusiasts find assurance in the family formation rate and omit the necessity for capital. Capital cannot be assumed. It must be provided for, something we are not doing. Largely because of confiscatory taxation, capital accumulation is falling behind the growth of population. The next generation may have to share want instead of abundance.

Spokesmen for stabilizers also find assurance in some $200 billion in "liquid savings" in the country, which will act as a "cushion" to any decline. But the $200 billion has been already largely loaned in the more than $640 billion national public and private debt. If the individual and corporate depositors wish to spend their "savings" they must get it from the banks. The banks in turn must get it from their debtors, public and private. In the words of Henry Hazlitt: "One man's quick asset is usually somebody else's quick liability. Considered individually, people have savings. But *collectively* they cannot spend their savings—for the simple reason that these have already been spent."

On balance, where are the economic stabilizers taking us? All of them represent some variation of the dubious purchasing power theory and, with the exception of unions, involve public spending, usually deficit spending. An old "solution." Public spending did not work in the Great Depression, however convincing [were] the pump-priming arguments of Keynes (the multiplier effect and the acceleration principle) to many economists. . . .

The business cycle is unhappily not extinct. But its extremes of boom and bust can be avoided if the government ceases its intervention into the economy. Let the government encourage thrift and investment. Let the government permit the interest rate to find its natural level and thereby automatically balance production with consumption, savings with investment.

WHAT THE FUTURE HOLDS FOR BUSINESS

From an interview with Paul A. Samuelson. Reprinted from *U. S. News & World Report* (December 14, 1964.) Copyright © 1964 U. S. News & World Report, Inc.

1 According to Samuelson, what is the main reason a depression will not happen again?
2 How does Samuelson deal with the traditional argument for a balanced budget?
3 Do you agree with Samuelson that it is not the business of each family and each corporation to insure economic stability? Why or why not?

Q. [to Samuelson] Can you foresee a downturn leading to a severe depression?

A. I don't think we will ever have a depression such as that of the 1930's again. That is not because it is impossible, but because the probability of one is now so low that the prudent man ought to disregard that probability.

Q. Why is that? Is it because of built-in cushions, such as Social Security and unemployment insurance?

A. The built-in cushions play a very important role in enhancing the over-all stability of the system. But their primary function is to iron out the small waves in business activity. You could not prevent a 1930-type depression, if it ever developed, by the present unemployment-compensation system.

The insurance of bank deposits by the Government is an absolutely essential ingredient which could help very much to keep a private banking system from going down the way it did in the early 1930's.

But the main argument against further depressions is not in our technology. It's not in the attitude of the consumer. It's not in the attitude of business. The big change since the 1930's is this: In the last analysis, we will not sit by and do nothing when a chronic slump is developing and threatens to feed upon itself. The Government, in a democracy, can step in to turn the tide. All the political pressures these days are for making the Government take those steps.

Q. What steps can the Government take to keep the economy prosperous?

A. There is no simple formula. But I do think we need a rational attitude toward tax-and-spending policy, and toward policies on interest rates and the supply of money. We didn't have that until about four years ago. Experience in the last couple of years suggests to me that the American people and their political leaders have adopted a much more rational attitude toward these things.

Q. Can you explain what you mean by a more rational attitude?

A. I mean that the end-all of fiscal soundness is not a balanced budget in each and every year. I mean that the end-all of money policy is not the cheapest money and the lowest interest rates, in season and out.

It means that we handle our over-all tax revenues and over-all Government spending with due regard to the level of unemployment. When capital spending and consumer spending are languid, we should lean against the wind and reduce the Government's intake of tax revenues and/or expand spending by the Government.

Conversely, when the private economy at the consumer and corporate level is overexuberant in its expenditures, budget policy must go into reverse. To lean against the inflationary wind, there must be an increase in tax revenues and/or a reduction in Government expenditures. This is the notion of tax-and-spending policy as a balance wheel.

Q. What, specifically, is needed to keep the economy strong in the next few years?

A. A higher level of total demand and spending for goods and services is indispensable. This could come if business spends more for plant and equipment than they now plan. It could come if the consumer saves not 7.5 per cent of his income, but only 6.5 per cent and spends the difference. . . .

A greater emphasis on tax cuts means a decision to use our resources for private consumption of goods, just the way every family spends its disposable income. An increase in federal and State expenditures means a decision to use part of our fruits of growth for collective social purposes—air-pollution control, education, things that concern us all. . . .

There's nothing sacred about the 100-billion-dollar spending level for the Federal Government, or any other level.

Q. Should tax cuts or increased Government spending be considered only as means to counter a downturn?

A. Not at all. Consider the important concept of "fiscal drag" which you will be hearing a lot about in the months to come. It has nothing directly to do with recession at all.

Q. What do you mean by "fiscal drag"?

A. If the American economy succeeds in growing at a 4 per cent rate, the existing tax structure will raise an extra 6 to 7 billion dollars per year. Built-in increases in Government spending—pay raises, and so on—are not that great. We certainly won't stand by and let this fiscal drag by the Government choke off the prosperity of the system.

That is why future tax cuts, future expenditure increases, or future sharing of revenue with the States is likely to be in the cards—recession or not. . . .

Q. With all the actions that Government can take, is it possible for the economy to keep going up continually? Must we have any pauses at all?

A. In this country, we regard a growth rate of 4 per cent as par for the course. But sometimes you'll be running at 5 and 6 per cent, and you will have overdone things a bit. As a result, you will develop inflationary pressures and something will have to be done about them. When that something is done, you are likely to have a pause.

In addition, investment opportunities are in the lap of the gods. They depend upon technological change, upon bright ideas and inventions, upon changes in consumers' tastes. If people suddenly like the new automobile models, as they did in 1955, you get a sprint. After that sprint is over, you have a period of relaxation. When this happens in a number of industries simultaneously, you tend to get a pause.

Q. Does this mean that if business and consumers could learn to be more reasonable and—

A. I think people are very reasonable and rational. I've never believed in the crime-and-punishment theory of the business cycle— that we lived too high in the 1920's or the early 1950's and therefore we had to go through seven long years of want and scarcity.

It's not the business of each family to insure the stability of the U.S. economy. It's not the business of each corporation to insure this stability. We can all make our contribution. But, in the last analysis, the flywheel or the governor on our system is the Federal Reserve System and its policy on credit and money, and the Congress and the executive branch in its tax and spending policies. That's what must be relied on for over-all stabilization.

Q. How does your idea of the role of Government square with the goal of a balanced budget?

A. It is quite incompatible with the notion of a balance each day, each month, each year. It is more compatible with a balance in the budget over the so-called business cycle, lasting a period of years. But, even there, economic conditions could arise so that the budget should not be balanced even over a complete business cycle.

Q. But if we can't balance the budget during record levels of activity, as we have had during the past few years, when will we ever balance it?

A. It is true that this year we have done better than last year, and that last year was better than the year before. But one of the most naïve notions still left in discussions of the American economy is the notion that, if you do better than last year, you're establishing records. Par for the course is not just to have the highest consumption ever. Par for the course is to have about 4 per cent higher consumption this year than you had last year. . . .

Q. In other words, we haven't performed well enough in the

past few years to warrant pushing the budget into a surplus position—

A. Exactly.

DOES MONETARY HISTORY REPEAT ITSELF? THE PRESENT & THE PAST

Abridged from "Does Monetary History Repeat Itself?" by William McChesney Martin, Jr. from VITAL SPEECHES OF THE DAY (July 15, 1965). Reprinted by permission of City News Publishing Co.

1 According to Martin, what are some of the similarities between the 1920's and the present?

2 Do you agree with Martin's observation that "the severity of the great depression was largely due to the absence of prompt anti-recession measures"? Why or why not?

When economic prospects are at their brightest, the dangers of complacency and recklessness are greatest. As our prosperity proceeds on its record-breaking path, it behooves every one of us to scan the horizon of our national and international economy for danger signals so as to be ready for any storm.

Some eminent observers have recently compared the present with the period preceding the breakdown of the interwar economy, and have warned us of the threats of another great depression. We should take these warnings seriously enough to inquire into their merits and to try to profit in the future from the lessons of the past.

And indeed, we find disquieting similarities between our present prosperity and the fabulous twenties.

Then, as now, there had been virtually uninterrupted progress . . . . And if we disregard some relatively short though severe fluctuations, expansion had been underway for more than a generation—the two longest stretches of that kind since the advent of the industrial age; and each period had been distorted in its passage by an inflationary war and postwar boom.

Then, as now, prosperity had been concentrated in the fully developed countries, and within most of these countries, in the industrialized sectors of the economy.

Then, as now, there was a large increase in private domestic debt; in fact, the expansion in consumer debt arising out of both residential mortgages and installment purchases has recently been much faster than in the twenties.

Then, as now, the supply of money and bank credit and the turnover of demand deposits had been continuously growing; and while in the late twenties this growth had occurred with little overall change in gold reserves, this time monetary expansion has been superimposed upon a dwindling gold reserve.

Then, as now, the Federal Reserve had been accused of lack of flexibility in its monetary policy: of insufficient ease in times of economic weakness and of insufficient firmness in times of economic strength.

Then, as now, the world had recovered from the wartime disruption of international trade and finance, and convertibility of the major world currencies at fixed par values had been restored for a number of years.

Then, as now, international indebtedness had risen as fast as domestic debt . . . .

Then, as now, the payments position of the main reserve center—Britain then and the United States now—was uneasy, to say the least . . . .

Then, as now, some countries had large and persistent payments surpluses and used their net receipts to increase their short-term reserves rather than to invest in foreign countries.

Then, as now, the most important surplus country, France, had just decided to convert its official holdings of foreign exchange into gold, regardless of the effects of its actions on international liquidity. . . .

And most importantly, then as now, many Government officials, scholars, and businessmen were convinced that a new economic era had opened, an era in which business fluctuations had become a thing of the past, in which poverty was about to be abolished, and in which perennial economic progress and expansion were assured. . . .

In my judgment, it is less fruitful to look for institutional changes or for a semiautomatic mechanism that would guarantee perennial prosperity than to draw from interwar experience some simple lessons that could save us from repeating our worst mistakes.

First, most observers agree that to a large extent the disaster of 1929-33 was a consequence of maladjustments born of the boom of the twenties. Hence, we must continuously be on the alert to prevent a recurrence of maladjustments—even at the risk of being falsely accused of failing to realize the benefits of unbounded expansion. Actually, those of us who warn against speculative and inflationary dangers should return the charge: our common goals of maximum production, employment, and purchasing power can be realized only if we are willing and able to prevent orderly expansion from turning into disorderly boom.

Second, most observers agree that the severity of the great depression was largely due to the absence of prompt anti recession measures. In part, the necessary tools for this were not then available nor were their potentialities fully understood. Today it is easy to understand where observers went wrong 35 years ago. But it is less easy to avoid a repetition of the same mistake; we always prefer to believe what we want to be true rather than what we should know to be true. Here again, we need most of all eternal vigilance. But we must also be ready to admit errors in past judgments and forecasts, and have the courage to express dissenting even though unpopular views, and to advocate necessary remedies.

Third, and most importantly, most observers agree that the severity of the great depression was due largely to the lack of understanding of the international implications of national events and policies. Even today, we are more apt to judge and condemn the worldwide implications of nationalistic actions taken by others than to apply the same criteria to our own decisions.

Recognition of the close ties among the individual economies of the free world leads to recognition of the need to maintain freedom of international commerce. This means . . . we must avoid any impairment of the value and status of the dollar. . . .

It should not have taken the great depression to bring these simple truths home to us. Today, as we approach the goal of the Great Society—to make each of our citizens a self-reliant and productive member of a healthy and progressive economic system—we can disregard these truths even less than we could a generation ago. By heeding them instead, we will have a good chance to avoid another such disaster. If monetary history were to repeat itself, it would be nobody's fault but our own.

WHY RECESSIONS ARE OBSOLETE

Abridged from "Why Recessions Are Obsolete" by Robinson Newcomb. © 1965, Nation's Business—the Chamber of Commerce of the United States. Reprinted from the May issue.

1 According to Newcomb, how does diversity of the economy protect against recession?

2 According to Newcomb, what change in the nature of employment in the United States has helped to make a depression unlikely?

3 Do you agree with Newcomb that the changing pattern of consumer spending has made for greater economic stability? Why or why not?

Our economy today is all but recession-proof.

There's no reason why business, now riding high into the fifth year of our greatest boom, should worry about a sharp dip in the future.

For five major reasons it now appears that we have about blocked the plunges in the business cycle we dreaded in the past:

1. Our economy is protected against recession by its diversity.

2. Major sources of jobs have become steady.

3. People are spending much more for many more things.

4. Government is adopting a new approach.

5. Business is wiser now.

The U.S. economy of 1965 is amazingly diversified. No single industry dominates the economy.

If one, or even a few industries, dominated the economy, even minor fluctuations in these industries could cause trouble. When the demand for or price of copper falls, for example, Chile is in trouble. Ghana is in serious difficulty when the price of cocoa is low. But when no industry is dominant, several industries can lose business without affecting us seriously. Other industries can be picking up steam at the same time these are slacking off.

Depressions and recessions in the United States during the

Nineteenth Century were very heavily influenced by the fact that the U.S. economy was dominated by agriculture. When the foreign market for agricultural products was weak, we had trouble. When it was strong, we had prosperity. Almost as much may have been sold abroad then as was sold for domestic nonfarm consumption.

The move towards diversification has been a long, slow process. Its importance in reducing business fluctuations has been glimpsed only dimly.

Manufacturing accounted for about one sixth of all employment a century ago. It is over 25 per cent today.

Trade, our next largest employer, accounted for only one eighth of total employment as late as 1909. Services, our third largest employer, accounted for only 10 per cent of all employment a century ago. It is now over 20 per cent.

Government is our fourth largest employer. It accounted for about two per cent of the total a century ago. Government now hires one out of every seven workers. These major groups provide two thirds of all employment now instead of the single uncertain occupation farming did 150 years ago.

No group outside of manufacturing, trade, services and farming now accounts for as much as 10 per cent of all employment. Employment is so widely dispersed now that it takes a major reversal which affects almost everything to cause serious economic difficulty.

Even the sources of employment are widely diversified within themselves. Manufacturers make everything from military hardware to milady's hat.

A second reason we can look for increased economic stability is the fact that all but one of our major sources of employment now have relatively steady markets. Even agricultural income is relatively steady. . . .

Manufacturing, of course, has replaced agriculture as the major source of employment. Yet manufacturing and agriculture combined account for only 35 per cent of all jobs.

Consumer markets have grown and diversified. And as income rises, people naturally buy more things. But they don't just buy more of the same things. They buy a greater variety.

This diversification in consumer spending has been increasing faster than incomes have risen. . . .

Because many things now compete for the consumer's dollar, the chance that he will cut his purchases is reduced.

The old classroom concept of value was that the first orange might have considerable value to the consumer, but after he had eaten one, the second orange was less enticing, the third orange might be satiating, and fourth one repugnant. This was thought to prove that consumers' desires were limited.

If his income went up his expenditures did not go up proportionately, the theory went, but his savings went up more than proportionately. This could mean that as incomes rose, savings would rise, the proportion of income spent would drop, and soon industry and workers would be out of jobs.

We now know this is false. If you have all the oranges you want, you take in a show or buy a new necktie. Psychological studies show that consumers' appetites increase with feeding. . . .

Even when income drops, many types of spending continue. A general confidence in the future, now widespread, encourages families to try to maintain their standard of living. They may postpone buying a new refrigerator if the expected salary raise doesn't come through, and buy the same cuts of steak and take the same trips. Only if they are sure they will have a lower income in the future, or will not be able to regain their former income, will they begin cutting back on non-durables. So demand tends to hold up through economic slowdowns.

This is very important, because consumer expenditures represent 63 per cent or more of the total value of goods and services produced. Consumer expenditures have risen every year since 1933. This greatly bolsters the whole economy. . . .

Government is now a source of economic stability for several reasons.

First, government spending for goods and services now comprises 20 per cent of the economy.

State and local expenditures are rising and will continue to rise, not only absolutely but also as a proportion of the whole economy.

While federal purchases of goods and services have been declining as a proportion of the total economy since 1958, state and local outlays have been rising as fast or faster than federal expenditures decline. This trend is likely to continue. State and local expenditures do not fluctuate as do federal outlays. They rise a bit more rapidly in some years than in others, but they are generally a stabilizing influence. . . .

Another major force on the business cycle occurs when there is a unanimous or near unanimous decision on the part of businessmen to speculate in one form or another. . . .

If industry as a whole goes on a speculative binge, and the government takes the wrong action, the trouble can be accentuated.

Despite these errors of judgment in 1955-58, consumer, farm and government expenditures rose. While business investment went down by $11 billion, the rise elsewhere in the economy was such that national production in 1958 was only 1.5 per cent less than in 1957.

With government buying 20 per cent of what the economy produces, consumer outlays of 63 per cent, and agriculture adding another five per cent, there's a broad, dependable base of nearly 90 per cent of the economy.

The ten per cent or so left is business investment. Much of this investment is stable.

Private residential construction has dropped at times, particularly when the government intervened. But in general the basic housing market today is strong and rising. Household formation is rising. . . .

So it now takes an overriding outside pressure on the economy to bring a recession. This pressure can come from the government, from the Federal Reserve Board, from industry as a whole if it goes on a speculative spree, or from a real abuse of organized labor's powers.

Mistakes will be made, but they may not have serious impacts on more than about five per cent of the economy.

QUESTIONS FOR CLOSER STUDY

1 On the basis of your reading, justify or refute the following statement: "While recessions are possible, severe depressions are unlikely."

2 If a depression were to occur, which of the stabilizers

discussed in the readings would reduce the effects on the individual?

3 Which stabilizers might be most effective in stimulating business and trade?

4 What do you think are some of the underlying causes of the business cycle?

5 Do you think that saving money during a "boom" would help individuals and businesses to survive a "bust"? Why or why not?

CHAPTER 10

WHAT SHOULD BE
THE ROLE OF
GOVERNMENT IN
THE ECONOMY?

The question of the role of government in the economy of the United States is older than the Republic. During the colonial period the British government tried to control the economic life of the Americans by imposing repressive trade and tax laws and by banning the manufacture of goods that competed with those produced in Great Britain. The colonists' increasing opposition to these unpopular moves was one of the chief causes of the fight for independence.

But independence from Great Britain did not end all disputes over centralized economic controls. Some American leaders, such as Alexander Hamilton, insisted that economic stability and growth of the new republic depended on a strong central government. Others, such as Thomas Jefferson, argued that republican democracy could survive only if there were strong local governments.

Economic conditions in the United States are far different today than in Revolutionary times, when most Americans were relatively self-sufficient farmers. The debate then was over such issues as a single national money system and federal taxation of imports. Today the United States is a highly industrialized country where sides are taken on how much power the federal government should have in such fields as prices, wages, education, and civil rights.

When economic issues are debated in the United States today, most disputants argue within the framework of a private enterprise economy. That is, they debate the question: To what extent should government become involved in an economy that is, and should remain, largely privately owned and operated?

The readings in this chapter respect the limitations of this debate, discussing whether the United States government should be an active participant, an umpire, or a benevolent observer.

The first selection is from a speech given by Governor George Romney of Michigan to a Republican party gathering in November 1965. Romney, former president of American Motors, warns that the private enterprise system is threatened by increasing government intervention.

The second reading is from an article by Kenneth Watson, director of the Religion and Labor Council of America. It was published in 1963. Watson criticizes businessmen who oppose government controls because "they are against the will of God," yet fail to meet their own social responsibilities.

The third article is from a speech made by Henry Ford II to the National Retail Merchants Association in January 1967. Ford speaks strongly in favor of a partnership between business and government in meeting the nation's needs.

The last reading is from an article published in 1963 by economist James Tobin. In defending the administration of President

174

John F. Kennedy, Tobin insists that government is properly and deeply committed to establishing economic policy.

OUR UNIQUE ECONOMIC PRINCIPLES

Abridged from "Our Unique Economic Principles" by George Romney from VITAL SPEECHES OF THE DAY (November 23, 1965). Reprinted by permission of City News Publishing Co.

1 Does Romney consider industry-wide collective bargaining good or bad? Why?
2 What does Romney mean when he says, "The biggest inflationary force in America today is the government of the United States"?
3 What does Romney think will be the political results of what he calls "economic absolutism"?

[W]e are witnessing the gradual destruction of the free American economy, through the gradual destruction of the principles which have made it grow.

We are allowing them to be destroyed at the very moment that a few other nations are picking them up and using them to rise to new heights of prosperity and opportunity.

What are our basic and unique economic principles? Here are four.

First, the principle of competition. Enterprises compete with one another for the favor of the customers—just as political parties compete for the favor of the voters. This puts the heat on businessmen to offer better products at more attractive prices. It gives the people the power of choice. As a result, customers rule the marketplace and business. . . .

Second, the principle of voluntary cooperation. Competition would produce jungle conditions if free management and free labor had not exercised self-restraint and voluntary cooperation to help solve the problems which result from their activities. Selfish rugged individualism does not pay in the long run. It is enlightened individualism that makes cooperation possible, and it is cooperation that makes enlightened individualism possible.

Third, the principle of incentive, we believe that men shall be rewarded on the basis of their contribution. Everybody works harder because of incentive. Production goes up. Quality goes up. Customers benefit—and so do workers and employers.

And fourth, the principle of progress-sharing. We have divided the fruits of economic progress among customers, workers, and owners. Customers should benefit through good products, reasonable prices, increased purchasing powers, and higher standards of living. Workers should benefit through sharing in increased productivity that provides higher wages and better working conditions. And owners should benefit through increased sales that make possible greater profits at better prices, and permit greater investment in improved facilities, which in turn will bring increased productivity and better returns on investment. . . .

These four—competition, voluntary cooperation, reward based on contribution, and progress-sharing—are the basic principles which are the strength of the American economy. And these are the principles which are being bludgeoned to death today, in the name of a spurious "national interest" which is really only a cloak for short-run political expediency.

It is right and proper for the people, through their government, to protect and extend these principles. We have done so in the past—through anti-trust laws, labor and collective bargaining legislation, and governmental fiscal and monetary controls. But we have turned down a wrong road—the road to economic absolutism.

In the first place, our labor laws to promote desirable collective bargaining went too far. They did help to eliminate abuses and inequality. They broke up an excessive concentration of political and economic power in industry, and provided a needed counterbalance. But they have developed fatal flaws.

One flaw is that our labor laws distort the principle of cooperation and team work between management and unions. The worker's primary interest is no longer in the survival and success of the enterprise he works for. His primary interest is in the union. . . .

Both employers and unions in many basic industries are organized on a monopolistic basis for collective bargaining. We have mistakenly removed wages—the biggest element of cost and price—from competition. It is one thing to remove the workers of a single enterprise from wage competition with each other, but it is quite another thing to remove wages in a whole industry from competition.

What's the result? Power concentrations grow. Wage rates are fixed without regard to competitive factors. Pattern-setting industries like steel and autos establish wage levels affecting the level of wage cost in our whole economy. Labor costs go up faster than increases in productivity. . . .

Either the American economy is going to keep plunging down the road of concentration of power, with the government continually stepping in and finally eliminating the collective bargaining responsibility of employers and unions, or we are going to have to put collective bargaining back on the same competitive basis as prices. . . .

Let me summarize, because I know this is not a simple subject . . . . Monopoly collective bargaining struggles between giant corporations and giant unions siphon off all the progress before any reaches the customer. The customer becomes the forgotten man economically, and this invites further governmental intervention. . . .

Where else have we gone wrong? We have allowed our government to turn its back on sensible monetary and fiscal policies. It is pumping inflation into the economy with easy money, easy credit, big new spending, and tax cuts to stimulate a boom on top of a boom.

The biggest inflationary force in America today is the government of the United States. . . .

I say the "new economics" is phony economics. Its end result is a totally controlled economy, dominated by a giant government controlling giant companies and giant unions. And it can't last. A day of reckoning will come. And when it comes, as before in history, the people will pay. . . .

With a centralized economic system where government calls the shots, there is less likelihood of small interruptions, but greatly increased danger of a massive collapse. If decisions were being made by free labor and free management under proven principles of progress, there would be more progress, less likelihood of massive collapse, and government itself would be in a better position to take corrective and compensatory measures. . . .

We can maintain prosperity and economic freedom, without inflation or collapse, only if we move forward to a consistent application of the basic economic principles that have given us more economic progress than any other people in the world: competition, cooperation, reward based on contribution, and progress-sharing — not conflict, monopoly, coercion, and White House control.

We must take economic decisions out of the White House and put them back where they belong: back in the marketplace subject to the free choice of free consumers; back at the bargaining table, through the free negotiations of individual companies and individual unions, both dedicated to advancing the fortunes of the common enterprise on which their livelihood depends; and back in the offices of competing businessmen, through price competition that puts a premium on sharing progress with the people as a whole. . . .

Only if America excels in productivity can it win the world struggle between communism and freedom.

Only if America wins that struggle can mankind's yearning for health, universal well-being, and peace be realized.

**THE MYTH OF
THE "AMERICAN WAY"**

By Kenneth Watson. Copyright ©
1963 Christian Century Foundation.
Reprinted by permission from the
March 13, 1963 issue of *The Christian Century.*

1 Does Watson feel that businessmen should conduct their businesses in their own self-interest? Why or why not?
2 Do you agree or disagree with Watson that "insistence on individual freedom in economic affairs seems a hollow demand"? Why?
3 According to Watson, how important is religion in determining American business ethics?

Many of us continue to hold that economic success, individualistic competition, hard work, thrift, the accumulation of wealth and the eschewal of luxuries are virtues that lead to the achievement of moral ends. For those who so contend it is easy to equate the unrestricted pursuit of economic self-interest with Christian ethics. The welding of the two has enabled many a Christian to pursue his economic self-interest without feeling guilty.

Most of us tend to look back for the ideal economic system to that which prevailed when numerous small-scale firms sold their products in competition with other sellers. There was no "market power"; small firms could not influence the market so long as they acted in isolation. Prices fluctuated freely in response to supply and demand, and no outside force such as government was needed to control the flow. . . .

Today we have achieved a mixed economy, in which the determining influences are exerted by government, large-scale business and labor unions. Except for a small section of the economy, operations of the market place no longer fluctuate freely in response to supply and demand; rather, they are "administered," with the capacity to set prices in the hands of large-scale businesses. . . .

What we have had has been an economic creed that related the concept of the free market to the moral laws of religion, that insisted on the gold standard as the only possible basis for a currency system, that tolerated only limited government regulation—in general, one that insisted that our economic life be "free." This is 19th century thinking. Why do the majority of our people—businessmen in particular—cling to the classical creed, ignoring or failing to recognize how today's market place actually operates? . . .

One reason may be found in the ambiguity of the businessman's role in the American economic system. On one hand he feels that he must act in terms of self-interest or give way to a more effective performer. On the other, he is aware that while profit-oriented activities are tolerated by law and sanctioned by our social mores, self-interest is generally looked on as unworthy motivation. . . . He finds in it a set of beliefs, doctrines and symbols to help him fulfill his role in a business-oriented society. Thus even when he recognizes that a given action is unjust, unfriendly, nonsocial or even antisocial, he can take refuge in the myth that not to carry out that action would give the edge to his business rivals. He is convinced that he is but an agent of impersonal forces which limit his power to do what is right, that what he must do is determined by the whim of the autonomous consumer. And, making the myth even more acceptable, he can proclaim that "service" is an inevitable by-product of the pursuit of profit.

It would be better for the public and for the businessman himself if he would acknowledge that there is an inherent strain in his position, a natural conflict in the role he must play in the American economic system, and that there is no perfect method of resolving that conflict. . . .

The conflict that besets the businessman is no greater and the strain no more unbearable than that imposed on men who fill other responsible jobs. No 19th century ideology can help him reduce the tensions and anxieties inherent in his role. At least one of his fears would be reduced if he would recognize that few are quarreling with him. Some of us do, however, consider it necessary to understand our economic system and to try to determine where it is going—but such efforts do not threaten the businessman. Certainly most of us do not object to the material benefits which the operations of our economic system have brought us. This does not mean, however, that we approve slowness of economic growth or unemployment, or that we are happy with a system which permits goods to be in surplus supply while some people in our country are in dire need. . . .

The myth is perpetuated, too, by those who attempt continually and methodically to identify the Christian religion with the economic ideology of Adam Smith, and to call the product of this spurious wedding the "American Way." . . .

For most of us the boiling point is reached when we observe the effort of those who champion this view to identify the classical version of the American business creed as "Christian." The practice violates all we have learned about the error of identifying any particular social system with the will of God or with the "kingdom" of God. When economic and religious conservatives insist on such identification they are imparting to the status quo a dangerous religious sanction. . . .

The economic realities of mid-20th century America are quite contrary to the economic model espoused by those who perpetuate the "free enterprise" myth. Our present system depends on and revolves around the operations of a relatively few large corporations. Reputable economists tell us that determination of the nation's strength and purpose lies in the hands of a few thousand men who control the bureaucracies—a few hundred only—which dominate our economy. . . .

Whether or not the wealthy are in a "great dark conspiracy" to run the country, present economic reality does raise grave moral and ethical problems. . . . The basic issue has to do with the conception of man as an economic being. Since John Calvin and Adam Smith, economic theory has been based on a psychological-theological image of man, with priority given to his freedom as an individual. But insistence on individual freedom in economic affairs seems a hollow demand when we are confronted by 20th century economic fact. . . .

It is incumbent upon the forces of religion to continue their protests against that immorality. For if the propagandists of economic conservatism continue to dull the moral issue and to identify God's will with theirs without being challenged, the forces of religion will become immobilized, impotent to help stem the major conflict looming on the social and economic scene.

BUSINESS AND GOVERNMENT: WHICH SHOULD DO WHAT?

Abridgment of "Business and Government: Which Should Do What?" a speech by Henry Ford II, delivered at the National Retail Merchants Association in New York. Reprinted by permission of Ford Motor Company

1 According to Ford, what is the main problem in government-business relations?
2 Do you agree or disagree with the analogies Ford uses in defending business advertising and bank-deposit interest rates? Why?
3 How much responsibility do you think institutions of society—other than business and government—should have for meeting the nation's problems?

[It is] my conviction that the relations between government and business have been changing in basic ways and for basic reasons—ways and reasons that affect all business and should be considered carefully by all businessmen.

The most obvious aspect of this change is the rapid penetration of government into all the activities of business. This, too, may sound familiar, but I think you would all agree that government involvement in business has been expanding more rapidly in recent years than at any time since the 1930's. . . .

The progress of science and technology has given us the material resources to accomplish unprecedented tasks—to reach the moon, to fight a good-sized war and to raise our standard of living simultaneously. Moreover, our capacity to solve the most difficult problems has been vastly enlarged by advances in computer science, in new problem-solving methods and in our knowledge of man and society.

The inevitable result of our growing ability to reach new goals has been the raising of our national sights. If we can reach the moon—then why can't we abolish poverty? If we can have both guns and butter, then why can't we also have safe highways, clean air, pure water, honest advertising, full employment, competent auto mechanics, stable prices, peaceful labor relations, good television programs and all the other things that go to make a great society?

Of course, there are good reasons why we can't solve all our problems all at once. One of them is that the combination of rising affluence and rising population multiplies our problems along with our problem-solving capacities. More people driving more cars more miles means more traffic congestion, more parking problems, more highway accidents. More people consuming more goods of all kinds means more waste products to be disposed of in the only three available repositories—the air, the water, or the ground. Like Lewis Carroll's Alice, we must run faster and faster merely to stand still.

It seems clear, however, that the American people have no more patience with these new problems than they have with the older ones. The more progress our country makes, the more progress it demands. . . . [W]e expect more from life, and we are determined to get it. Barring some drastic set-back that saps our national confidence, I would expect Americans to go right on demanding more from life—and I, for one, would have it no other way.

To say that people expect more from life really implies

that they expect more from all the major institutions of society, including especially business and government. Business firms, government agencies and legislatures are all operating today under stricter and more demanding public standards than ever before.

By and large, I think both business and government have made a strong effort to respond to the national demand for progress on all fronts. As it happens, however, there are few major problems that can be solved by government alone, without business, or by business alone, without government.

Take your pick of the problems . . . —from poverty to traffic accidents, from water pollution to labor strife—not one of them is exclusively a governmental problem, nor exclusively a business problem. Each of them overlaps both areas by a very considerable margin.

Here, I think, is where we finally locate the basic source of the growth of government involvement in business affairs. As government and business both respond to the major problems of our day, as each of them enlarges the scope of its responsibilities to the public, they inevitably move into the no-man's-land where functions overlap and boundaries are ill-defined. And therefore they are bound to bump into each other more and more frequently, and more or less violently.

From all of this I draw two conclusions. First, the quality of business-government relations is crucial to the future progress of our nation. None of our major problems can be solved and none of our major goals can be reached unless business and government learn to pull together rather than at cross purposes.

My second conclusion is that there is really only one way to get business and government to pull together. To keep them from constantly colliding with each other as they work on common problems, we have to draw boundaries between them. We have to decide more rationally, more consistently and more clearly than we are now doing what functions and responsibilities belong to government, and what can better be left to private initiative.

It seems to me that there are two ways to go about making these distinctions.

The wrong way is what might be called the good guys vs. the bad guys approach. There are still a lot of businessmen—though, fortunately, fewer than there used to be—who think that the main difference between business and government is one of virtue and wisdom. From this point of view, the average government official is a bumbler, a bureaucrat, an opportunist or worse. Government, in short, is the enemy.

On the other hand, there are still a lot of government people —though again fewer than there used to be—who simply turn this assumption around. From their point of view, the average businessman is a selfish, shortsighted, ruthless profiteer. Business serves only private aggrandizement, while government serves only the public interest. Business, in short, is the enemy.

This may seem like a caricature, but it seems to me that most people in business and in government suffer at least a little bit—some of us a great deal—from the tendency to overlook our own failings and exaggerate those on the other side. We could all do with a bit more humility and a stronger effort to see ourselves as others see us.

When you come right down to cases, there is probably very little to choose between business and government on the score of virtue and wisdom. Let's take a few examples.

. . . [Y]ou and I know that the business world is intensely competitive. We must also admit that in the heat of competition, businessmen sometimes do things they shouldn't do, and leave undone some things they ought to do. That, after all, is why we need commercial law and regulatory agencies.

On the other hand, it's difficult to think of any business that is more competitive than politics. Like businessmen, legislators and government officials sometimes do things in the heat of competition that they should not do, and leave undone things they ought to do. If businessmen sometimes place short-run profit ahead of higher considerations, I suspect that once in a while politicians give greater weight to their own immediate political advantage than to the public interest.

. . . [A]utomobile advertising [has been criticized] because it is emotional and persuasive rather than coldly factual and informative. The use of pretty girls in car ads [has been] . . . especially deplored.

It seems to me there is a fair comparison to be made between business advertising and political campaigning. I don't re-call that I heard a single campaign speech last fall that consisted strictly of the facts, all the facts and nothing but the facts. It seems to me there were even a few pretty girls in some of the campaign parties. And I wonder when was the last time a political party made good on all the promises in its platform.

Just before Christmas, the four Federal agencies that regu-late banks sent a letter to all banks whose deposits are insured by the government. The letter banned misleading claims about in-terest rates paid on deposits. Among other things, the government instructed the banks to state the fact if an advertised rate of interest is payable only on accounts held for a specified length of time.

Then somebody asked an embarrassing question. What about government advertising of government savings bonds? Shouldn't the Treasury Department point out that bonds must be held for seven years to earn the advertised rate of 4.15 percent? Shouldn't it state that after one year the interest is only 2.24 percent?

The Treasury doesn't think so. In fact, an unnamed spokes-man was rather indignant at the suggestion. . . .

Defenders of consumer interests are very much concerned over the bewildering variety of items on the retailer's shelves these days. How, they ask, can the customer possibly choose wisely among so many similar products?

To get back to the last election, I was somewhat bewildered myself when I faced the voting machine, and I doubt that I really made all the wisest choices among all the similar candidates. It may be that something could be done to simplify both sets of choices, but it may also be that the difficulty is at least in part the price we pay for the right to choose.

The automobile manufacturers have taken their lumps for being slow to require all their customers to pay for safety features that the customers were not exactly eager to have. On the other hand, we in the industry think that governments have been slow to enforce the laws against drunken driving and to impose other unpopular traffic safety measures such as tighter driver licensing standards and compulsory vehicle inspection. Perhaps both sides have been guilty of expecting the other to take steps that are nec-essary, but risky. . . .

I think the point is evident. Neither business nor government has a monopoly on virtue and wisdom. Both are made up of fallible people who generally do their best in a mixed-up world. Sometimes they do well; sometimes not. But by and large American government and American business work reasonably well—better than in most other places, and better than they used to. . . .

By and large, government does well when it works in harmony rather than at cross purposes with the dynamic forces of free enterprise. By and large, it does well when it sets the broad rules of the game, and it does poorly when it seeks to control business activities in detail.

By and large, business does well when it sticks to what it knows best and has the strongest incentives for accomplishing. . . .

One . . . of the many things that businesses can do is support rather than oppose well-considered government programs to accomplish what government can do and business cannot do.

The real question for businessmen is not how to stop the growth of government. To meet our nation's growing problems and aspirations, both government and business must expand their responsibilities and activities. The only real question is which of them should do what.

**HOW PLANNED
IS OUR ECONOMY?**

Abridgment of "How Planned Is Our Economy" by James Tobin from THE NEW YORK TIMES MAGAZINE, October 13, 1963. Copyright © 1963 by The New York Times Company. Reprinted by permission.

1 According to Tobin what are some of the direct controls that the U.S. government has imposed on the economy since World War II?
2 How do direct controls and indirect controls differ?
3 Do you agree with Tobin that the steel-price episode of April 1962 showed that the Kennedy administration was trying "to defend the dollar *without* new controls"? Why or why not?

Like the New Deal and Fair Deal before it, the New Frontier has provoked shrill warnings that an "anti-business" Administration seeks to supplant the "free-enterprise system" with a "planned economy." . . .

The Kennedy Administration has been puzzled and hurt to find itself cast in this role. Unlike its Democratic predecessors, the New Frontier leaned over backward to avoid earning an "anti-business" label and to forestall suspicions that it contemplated radical changes in U.S. economic institutions. Evidently there is still considerable misunderstanding—between the Administration and its critics, and in the public at large—about the role of government policies and plans in a private enterprise economy such as ours.

To what extent can and does the Federal Government plan and control the American economy? . . .

[Direct] government controls over the activities of specific business firms and individuals—specifying the quantities of materials they can buy and stock, the kinds and quantities of goods they can produce, the amounts they can or must sell to different customers, the prices they may or must charge—are familiar to the American people from the Second World War. No one in his right mind wishes to revive the battery of war-time controls unless another full-scale military mobilization is forced upon us.

A few controls, some Federal, others state and local, are permanently scattered over the peacetime economic landscape. These are quite a mixed bag. Some, like the strengthened drug legislation adopted in the wake of the thalidomide scare, are meant simply to safeguard public health or safety. The rates and services of public utilities are regulated, on the grounds that customers of . . . monopolies lack the automatic protection of competition. Elsewhere, some direct government interventions, like those under the anti-trust laws, are intended to preserve or restore competition. . . .

The major indirect controls are Federal expenditures and receipts. . . .

Government expenditures affect, first of all, the economic fortunes of the individuals and businesses who actually receive the Government checks. But as the initial recipients respend the money, Government outlays are quickly and widely diffused over the whole country. Consequently an increase in Federal expenditures, whatever its initial purpose and distribution, is an injection of general purchasing power into the economy. Just like injections of purchasing power from private sources, a rise in Federal spending tends to increase sales, jobs, incomes, profits, and sometimes prices, throughout the economy.

On the other side . . . taxes drain purchasing power from the economy. Higher taxes affect first of all the taxpayers on whom they are levied. But the reduction in their ability to spend spreads to the whole economy, generally reducing sales, jobs, incomes, profits and sometimes prices. . . .

The other main "indirect control" is monetary policy. Under the Constitution the Federal Government has the inescapable power and responsibility of a central government "to coin money, regulate the value thereof."

As the economy has developed, bank checks have supplanted coins and paper currency as the usual means of payment. The Government therefore has acquired, mainly through the Federal Reserve Act of 1913, significant control of the aggregate volume of bank deposits and bank credit. Banks are required to hold a certain percentage of their deposits as reserves, either in vault cash or on deposit with Federal Reserve Banks. . . .

Not even the most doctrinaire advocate of laissez-faire favors free enterprise in the minting of coins or the printing of paper currency; and few would argue that the quantity of bank-created money can safely be left to unfettered competition among private banks. There is no escape from the fact that the Government possesses and must exercise monetary powers over the economy. . . .

But does not the dramatic steel-price episode of April, 1962, prove that the Administration seeks to substitute government controls for private decisions? It proves, if anything, the opposite, for the Administration's actions were part of a determined effort to defend the dollar *without* new controls. . . .

. . . [B]oth Presidents Eisenhower and Kennedy have agreed on the principles of noninflationary wage and price behavior. Both Presidents have tried to throw the moral weight of the Presidency and of public opinion on the side of restraint in wage negotiations and price decisions. Nevertheless, as many recent events demonstrate, these decisions remain in private hands.

The Government has been involved, one way or another, in

every labor-management dispute and settlement in steel since the war. No Administration can regard a stoppage in so basic an industry as a purely private concern to which the Government is indifferent. . . .

In 1962, the Kennedy Administration sought to encourage the parties to reach a new steel labor contract without a strike well before the June 30 deadline. But, as the President had made clear to everyone as early as the previous September, the Administration did not seek peace at any price level. The President . . . sought a non-inflationary settlement, holding the wage increase within the range of productivity gains in order to permit stability in steel prices. . . .

. . . The ink was scarcely dry on the new contracts when U.S. Steel precipitated the famous . . . [steel price increase]. After using his moral influence to obtain moderation from the union, the President could scarcely have failed to speak out against the announced price increase.

The economic record of the New Frontier does not justify the dark suspicions and heated attacks of which it has been the target. Probably there is today a greater and more stable social consensus on the frontiers between government activity and private enterprise than at any time in this century.

No influential opinion . . . supports nationalization of any private industry. . . . No one . . . is seriously proposing massive government efforts to redistribute income and wealth. No one . . . seeks to use government power to shift the present balance of power between organized labor and management. No one seriously advocates any general extension of the list of direct government controls over the economic activities of individuals and business firms. These may have been the great issues that aroused the ideological battalions in the past, but they are not very relevant today.

Plenty of issues remain. But they are not for the most part questions of widening or narrowing the sphere of government activity. Rather they are differences of view about national priorities among various government activities—defense, space, education, etc.—and between public and private uses of economic resources. Or they concern the best use of existing government powers to achieve full employment, stability and economic progress. . . .

For surely it is a proper concern of the Government whether the economy is in recession or prosperity, whether unemployment is 7 per cent or 4 per cent of the labor force, whether prices are rising or reasonably stable, whether the dollar is weak or strong abroad, whether the gross national product is $500 [billion] . . . or $600 billion, and whether the G.N.P. is, on average, growing at 2 1/2 or 4 1/2 per cent per year. If conscious and coherent policy to discharge these responsibilities is "planning," then the Administration is guilty.

QUESTIONS FOR CLOSER STUDY

1 Which readings do you think were the most objective? the least objective? Why?

2 What controls over the economy do you think are best left to business and which to government? Why?

3 What kind of government controls do you think would be favorable to business interests but obnoxious to labor?

4 Which group do you think the government sides with more—business or labor? Why?

5 Defend or attack the statement: "Businessmen are selfish, shortsighted profiteers."

6 Defend or attack the statement: "Government officials are bumbling, dictatorial opportunists."

CHAPTER 11

CAN
MASS STARVATION
BE PREVENTED?

People starve. Young people die of diseases caused by vitamin deficiencies. People are stunted both physically and mentally because they cannot get enough of the right kinds of food or because they do not know how to use the food that they have. The problem exists in India. It exists in the Congo and Bolivia and Egypt. It exists in the United States. How serious a world problem is this? And how shall it be solved?

In calculating whether or not *mass* starvation is a possibility, economists must first determine the availability and allocation of resources and second, the means of distributing the fruits of production. The first consideration is complicated by conflicting statistics; the second leads to disputes over how economic systems should be organized, especially those of underdeveloped countries.

Thomas Robert Malthus in *Essay on the Principles of Population,* published in 1789, considered only the availability and use of resources. He argued that, although population theoretically should increase or decrease in proportion to the means of subsistence, a decline in the means of subsistence relative to uncontrollable growth in population is inevitable. Believing that man's choices in approaching such a decline are moral restraint or vice and misery—and that restraint is against human nature—Malthus forecast a terrible doom for the human race.

The Industrial Revolution, by expanding food production, and the Scientific Revolution, by providing new birth control measures, have destroyed conditions that would have fulfilled Malthus' prediction. However, many people, noting the global population explosion that has taken place since World War II, believe that its grim consequences may still be demonstrated in this century.

Conflicts between economic systems further complicate calculations as to whether or not mass starvation is a possibility. Some economists think that Malthus' theory is incomplete because it does not take into consideration the socio-economic systems under which a nation is likely to operate. These people insist that, despite the relative decline of food production, radically changing the nature of the economic system is enough to dispel the threat of mass starvation.

Thus, there are three answers to the possibility of mass starvation: 1) limit the birth rate; 2) increase food production to keep pace with population growth; or 3) radically change the socio-economic systems under which the people of the world live.

The first reading is a news story that appeared in *U.S. News & World Report*, October 4, 1965, supporting the contention that population growth exceeds present increases in food production. It states facts and trends that might result in mass starvation of the kind Malthus feared.

192

The second reading is by Dr. Daphne Chun, a member of the staff at Queen Mary Hospital in Hong Kong. Dr. Chun explains some of the successful techniques used in 1966 in Hong Kong to reduce population growth.

The third reading is by former Food and Agriculture Organization of the United Nations [FAO] nutritionist, Jean Mayer. Originally published in the magazine *Daedalus* in September 1964, it is critical of the prediction that world famine is a serious possibility. Mayer, hopeful that the world can support many more people, sees exciting possibilities in increased food production.

The last selection appeared in the Russian journal *Literaturnaya gazeta* on November 30, 1965. At that time its author, Ya. Guzevaty, was a graduate student in economics and a Soviet delegate to the second world conference on population problems. Recognizing that population growth has produced serious problems in the communist world, Guzevaty believes that the solution is in raising the socio-economic level of people in underdeveloped countries.

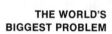
THE WORLD'S BIGGEST PROBLEM

Reprinted from U. S. NEWS & WORLD REPORT.

1 What is meant by the term "man-food ratio"?
2 In which areas of the world is the "population explosion" most apparent?
3 What is the relationship between the world's supply of essential fuels and industrial materials and the world's food supply?

In the next 35 years, the world's population, now about 3.3 billion, will skyrocket to about 6 billion—almost doubling by the year 2000.

Biggest population increases—more than 100 per cent—will come in the less developed nations, where population already is pressing severely against food supply.

Smallest increases—about 40 per cent—will come in the well-fed, industrial nations best able to handle growth. . . .

The world, even now, is facing a food problem. Diets are inadequate in the huge underdeveloped areas of the world, which include almost all of Asia and Africa and most of Latin America.

Just to maintain the present inadequate level of diet will require a virtual doubling of the world's output of food in the next 35 years.

This vast increase in food production must be achieved at a time when nearly all of the virgin lands of the world already have been brought into production.

There is no assurance that the job can be done in time.

Great famine, as a result, could be the outlook.

This warning is voiced by Dr. Earl L. Butz, dean of agriculture at Purdue University and onetime chairman of the U. S. delegation to the Food and Agriculture Organization of the United Nations .... But, it is asked: Hasn't the world always found a way to feed its ever-growing population?

The answer, according to the experts, is that the problem today is far more complex than at any time in the past.

For one thing, population growth is faster now—and getting faster all the time. Dr. Butz paints this picture:

"At the beginning of the Christian era, world population was estimated to have numbered around 250 million.

"In the next 16 centuries it doubled, reaching 500 million by 1600.

"Three centuries later, by 1900, world population had tripled, and stood at about 1.5 billion.

"In the less than two thirds of a century since 1900, world population has approximately doubled again.

"Reliable estimates indicate that in the little over one third of a century remaining until the year 2000, it will double again. . . .

"The astonishing fact is that the human race is currently doubling in numbers every 35 years. . . .

"Obviously, this rate of growth cannot persist indefinitely, because of the sheer limitation of space and food."

Complicating the problem is the fact that food production is not increasing as fast as the population. Dr. Butz reports this:

"The man-food ratio around the world, never high enough to be very exciting to two thirds of the world's population, has actually been in a decline the last half dozen years.

"Total food output has increased during those years, to be sure, but at a slower rate than population increase. In many of the world's underdeveloped areas, the man-food ratio is in a serious decline."

. . . The drama of the food problem that lies ahead will center in the following areas: Latin America, Asia, Africa.

Latin America's population in the next 35 years will zoom 157 per cent—from 245 million people now to 630 million people by the year 2000. . . .

Asia, which already holds 55 per cent of the world's population, is expected to show a rise of 89 per cent in population in the next 35 years—up from 1.8 billion now to about 3.4 billion in the year 2000. . . .

Asia's problem, loaded with potential for future tragedy, is where to find food for the 1.6 billion additional people that it must feed 35 years hence.

Or take the case of Africa, heading for a population growth of 151 per cent in the remainder of this century. . . . Africa, already importing food, faces the problem of feeding 466 added millions by 2000.

Taken all together, the "hungry" countries of the world— those considered by experts to have deficient diets—now contain about two thirds of the world's population but produce only about one third of the world's food. And it is almost exactly these hungry areas that face the biggest population growth in the years ahead. . . .

. . . One hopeful note is sounded by the experts: The world is not likely to run out of essential fuels or industrial materials in this century.

Reserves of coal, oil, gas and uranium will be adequate to provide increasing amounts of power for many years.

By the time uranium supplies run out—if they ever do—man will know how to extract energy from water.

Industry will have to turn to lower-grade sources of raw materials. But the ocean floor may yield large quantities of manganese, copper, nickel and cobalt. And plastics will be improved to replace metals in many uses.

. . . Water, in the crowded world of the future, looms as a

problem almost as serious as that of food. Sir John Cockcroft [winner of the Nobel Prize for physics in 1951 and now master of Churchill College at Cambridge, England] discusses the water situation in these words:

"Water supplies could be a limitation on the development of the economy, especially water supplies for industrial and agricultural use, since requirements are likely to double in the next 20 years. The future of Asia, Africa and Australia could be vitally affected by water shortage, and even in some parts of the United States this is becoming a problem. . . .

. . . Is there an answer to the world's biggest problem? Two things must be done, say the experts:

1. Increase food production greatly.
2. Reduce the world's birth rate.

"In the long run," says Dr. Butz, "say by the close of this century, birth control is the only solution."

But Dr. Shiroshi Nasu of Tokyo University warns: . . .

"As the adoption of birth control among the developing nations will presuppose a raised standard of living, a wider diffusion of general education as well as a changed mental outlook, it will certainly take many years to come. During this time, the predicted crisis will not stop approaching.

"It will be a race between the two, and our prospect of winning the race is not too bright at present.

"So we have to turn our attention toward the increase of food production."

. . . The United States, it is clear, will play a leading role in the coming battle to feed the world. . . .

On September 23, a new policy was proposed by Senator George McGovern (Dem.), of South Dakota, former Director of the Food for Peace program. He told the U.S. Senate:

"The most overwhelming paradox of our time is to permit half the human race to be hungry while we struggle to cut back on surplus production. . . .

"I believe that we ought to declare an all-out war against hunger. . . . We should announce to the world now that we have an unused food-producing capacity which we are willing and anxious to use to its fullest potential." . . .

196

Feeding a population the size of that foreseen by 2000 is going to be a job too big for any one country. Yet, for the U.S., says Dr. Butz: "There is no realistic alternative for us except to gear up to meet this challenge."

Copyright © 1965 U. S. News & World Report, Inc.

**A REVIEW OF CURRENT
FERTILITY CONTROL
ACTIVITIES
IN HONG KONG**

Abridged from "A Review of Current Fertility Control Activities in Hong Kong" by Daphne Chun M.D. from PLANNED PARENTHOOD-WORLD POPULATION (October 19, 1966). Reprinted by permission of the author and Planned Parenthood Federation of America, Inc.

1 Why is population growth a serious danger in Hong Kong?
2 Why can it be said that science is both helping solve and aggravating the population problem?
3 What are some of the methods used by the Family Planning Association to encourage family planning?

Economics must always be the servant of society. The greatest challenge to an orderly and healthy society today is the rapid increase in world population. Within the recent past, scientific and medical discoveries have so reduced the death rate that population expansion is threatening the well-being of all countries. In Hong Kong this is a serious problem indeed. The total land area is only 398 square miles, very little of it arable. There are barely any natural resources for livelihood and employment. We are dependent on trade and industry. How long can employment be found for everyone? Hong Kong is already an employer's market. Fifty per cent of the present population of almost 4,000,000 is under 19 years. The density of population, almost 10,000 per square mile, is also the highest in the world. The provision of education, health and medical services and housing, to mention only a few of the public services, are constantly overstrained to meet the demand made on them, yet according to [predictions] . . . our population will reach more than 4¾ million by the middle of 1971, barely five years hence.

In Hong Kong, as in every free community, we disagree with one another on many local issues—and rather enjoy doing so.

But, whatever our pet beliefs and theories may be, we are all agreed on one thing—that is that our exploding population poses a hidden time-bomb that could one day blow our economy apart. The answer to this imminent explosion is, fertility control. The task of fertility control fell at first solely on the Family Planning Association, a non-profit voluntary organization, as there was lack of official interest and no private organization undertook this work. For over ten years, the FPA has worked hard and has had considerable success. Their case list, which stood at 9,000 in 1956, has increased over seven fold to almost 66,000 in 1965. Within these ten years, the birth rate in Hong Kong decreased from 39.7 to 27 per 1000 last year. Had the birth rate continued at its 1955 level we would have had 143,000 born in 1965 instead of the 102,000 who were in fact born, a decrease of 41,000. A target, a major one, of the Association is to reduce further Hong Kong's birth rate to 20 per 1000 within 5 years. The expenditure of the Association for the past financial year was $168,600. The average outlay for each case, calculated on the expenditure against the number of patients treated, comes to about $2.50 per year.

The majority of our . . . population still have on the average of 6.5 in a family. Therefore, besides offering fertility control services, our efforts are also concentrated on impressing upon the parents the benefits and advantages of family planning. To achieve the former, there are at present 53 birth control clinics operating throughout Hong Kong, Kowloon and the New Territories. The number of women who attended these clinics in 1965 was 68,446. Their average age was 33, their average number of living children was 4, ranging from zero to seven. . . . Although the husbands' occupations covered a wide range, the majority (54%) were skilled laborers. This is the reverse of the trend in most Western countries where the professional classes tend to be more family planning minded. . . .

To arouse the interest of as many people as possible to practice family planning the Association engages in an active publicity campaign to make the public more aware of its work. Six one-minute color films were made last year and since May 1966 have [been] and are being shown at frequent intervals in 43 cinemas. Through this audio-visual means, we hope to impart the advantages of family planning to both the literate and illiterate. It has been estimated that these films can reach up to 2,000,000 people each month. Among other publicity activities are:

1. *Interviews.* During 1965, out of 35,946 new cases, 14,863 (41.4%) were referred by case workers following home visits. The impressive number of person-to-person contacts made during this period were mainly due to the additional help of 20 new field workers sponsored by the American Friends Service Committee, and the results confirm the importance of personal contacts. These workers were divided into teams, each consisting of four field workers under the supervision of one social worker, working in different areas by rotation, giving everyone the experience of working in villages, hospitals, clinics and resettlement areas.

2. *Broadcasts.* The number of radio broadcasts, interviews and programs amounted to 68, an increase of nearly 100% over 1964. A radio contest for a short play and theme song on family planning yielded a short drama titled "Family Planning" which was broadcast over Radio Hong Kong in ten series, each accompanied by the theme song. Spot announcements on family planning were broadcast over Commercial Radio and Rediffusion networks.

3. *News Releases and Advertisements.* The support from the press has been most encouraging to our work. 164 news articles and 34 special features (one-half or full page) were published in both Chinese and English newspapers. Ten Chinese newspapers and one English newspaper continued to grant special discounts for our advertisements.

4. *Film Shows.* In cooperation with various welfare agencies, organizations and factories, the Association arranged evening film shows for mothers' groups. On these occasions, our social/field workers also gave a talk on the benefits of family planning and our services. Altogether, our film, "A Story of Two Families" was shown 136 times to an audience of 25,400.

5. *Exhibitions.* The Association participated in the 23rd Annual Hong Kong Products Exhibition and the 4th Kaifong Medical and Health Exhibition. On both occasions interesting and well designed posters, charts and pamphlets were displayed. Field/Social workers were on duty at the booths, and many men and women asked for advice and information concerning birth control. More

than 120,000 pamphlets were distributed.

6. *Pamphlets & Posters.* 10,000 copies of five new posters . . . were printed and displayed at resettlement estates, hospitals, maternal and child health centers, factories, cinemas, etc., with the consent of the Government Information Service, the Labor Department, Medical Department and various other organizations. In 1965, 300,000 copies of 20 different pamphlets were printed and distributed.

7. *Contact with Families of Juvenile Court Cases.* Lists of names of children involved in juvenile court cases were received from the Justice of the Peace Courts with the request that our workers make personal visits to the parents of these children, since they are often from over-crowded homes. A total of 149 mothers were visited, of whom 40 (27½%) accepted advice to visit FPA clinics.

8. *Discussions.* Post-partum [after birth] discussions in hospitals, maternity clinics and private maternity homes were made from time to time. . . .

9. *Lectures.* Lectures and special talks on family planning and the work of the Association were given to hospital nurses, midwives, college students and staff members of welfare agencies, etc.

FOOD AND POPULATION: THE WRONG PROBLEM?

Reprinted with permission of DAEDALUS, Journal of the American Academy of Arts and Sciences, Boston, Mass. Summer 1964, "Population, Prediction, Conflict, Existentialism."

1 What criticism can be made of the author's statement that "the world will have a surplus of rice and wheat by 1975"? (Assume that his statement is an accurate prediction.)
2 What is a "food balance sheet"?
3 What does the title of the article mean?

World War II was not a Malthusian check: in spite of the horrendous numbers of soldiers and civilians killed, in spite of the massive genocide perpetrated by the Nazis, food production was decreased much more than population: by 1945 intake per capita was 16 per cent lower than the 1934-1938 average. . . . And yet very quickly the situation improved. The oil shortage vanished first; while the gigantic ground nut scheme of the British government, which was supposed to mitigate it, was taking off to a very slow start, the reappearance in the channels of trade of adequate amounts of fats and oils eliminated the motivation for the scheme itself. United States production of cereals and animal products, which had grown during the war in spite of lack of abundant manpower and the diversion of the chemical industry to military purposes, had to be slowed down as surpluses started accumulating, and, with their appearance, the threat of a collapse of agricultural prices loomed. By 1952-1953, the worldwide rate of per capita production of food had overtaken pre-war rates. Since then, the average rate of increase in the production of food for the world at large has been 3 per cent per year while the population has increased on the average 1.7 per cent. In document No. 8148, the Department of State estimates that if individual consumption levels remained at the 1955-1957 level, the world at large would show by 1975 an annual surplus of 40 million tons of wheat and 70 million tons of rice. . . .

. . . The food balance sheets on which postwar pessimism was based are imperfect instruments: [it is difficult] . . . to gauge such unknowns as figures for wasted food at the retail level and within families; that portion of the food supply which does not move within the channels of trade—the amount of food grown by the farmer for his family is very inaccurately known, particularly as regards fruits and vegetables, which tend to be underestimated. . . . [The] evolution of food balance sheets—the only instrument we have to judge the race between food and population—make it apparent that most regions do show the same slow increase of per capita supplies exhibited by the world at large. It must be recognized, of course, that many of the worst nutritional scourges of mankind have been historically due as much to ignorance and to callousness as to lack of nutrients as such. Thousands of children die of protein deficiency in areas where the proteins which would save them do in fact exist and are often consumed in sufficient amounts in the very household where infants and toddlers die for their lack: faulty understanding of the child's needs may be the main cause of his being denied some of the food consumed by his father and older siblings. As for man's inhumanity to man and its contribution to starvation, it could be illustrated by thousands of examples: from cereals being shipped from Ireland under the protection of naval guns during the famine to stocks being withheld during the Congo famine to keep prices up.

Certainly, as far as food is concerned, ours is not one world. The United States government rents twenty million acres from our farmers so that they will not grow food on them. A recent study made at Iowa State University suggests that sixty-two and a half million acres ought to be similarly retired so that surpluses will not continue to be created in relation to the present market. . . .

The present, bad as it is, is no worse than the past and probably somewhat better. But what of the future? In absolute numbers, the increase in population is likely to accelerate for some time. Can the food supply keep up? My contention is that, for better or for worse, it can and will.

First, let us consider conventional agriculture. FAO's figures indicate that 3.4 billion acres are at present under cultivation. This represents less than 11 per cent of the total land area of the world. A number of experts—Prasolov, Shantz, Zimmermann—estimate the area which can eventually be made arable at from 13 to 17 billion acres. Colin Clark, the director of the Agricultural Economics Research Institute of Oxford, uses the figure of 19 billion acres, but counts double-cropped tropical lands twice. (He considers, incidentally, that if the land were farmed as well as the Dutch farmers work their acres today, it would support 28 billion people on a Dutch diet; if Japanese standards of farming and nutrition were used, this area would support 95 billion people.)

The biggest potential increase of food production does not, however, come from the extension of the area under cultivation, but from the increase in the use of fertilizers. The phenomenal increase in food production in this country has actually been performed with a reduction in acreage farmed. By pre-World War I standards of cultivation, it took one-and-one-half acres to support an American. If such standards prevailed today, we would need to add at least 40 million acres to our farm area every ten years, or the equivalent of an additional Iowa every decade. In fact, we use the alternative—fertilizers. One ton of nitrogen is the equivalent of fourteen acres of good farmland. The use of between two and three hundred thousand tons of nitrogen (and corresponding amounts of other necessary elements) per decade has in fact obviated the need to discover another Iowa. Neither is our use of fertilizers as intensive as it is in Japan (where it is well over twice that employed here) or in Western Europe. (Incidentally, in spite of its already high standards of cultivation, Japan is still increasing its agricultural production at a rate of 3 per cent per year.) India, Africa, and most of Latin America use only an infinitesimal fraction of Japanese or Western amounts of fertilizer or use none at all. [Agricultural consultant, Jonathan] Garst has estimated that an expenditure of ten dollars an acre for fertilizers per year would alone add 50 to 100 per cent to the low yields in underdeveloped countries. Applying this investment to an area of 1.5 billion acres would be equivalent to adding at least 750,000,000 acres to the crop areas of these countries, the equivalent of a continent bigger than North America. It is interesting to note that this primacy of fertilizers was recognized relatively late. In this country, the recognition dates back only to World War II, and has accelerated since the Korean conflict. In Japan, it also dates back to 1950 or thereabout. And the leaders of the U.S.S.R. only last year realized that a large scale increase in fertilizer output would be easier and more rewarding than the extension of cultivation to the "virgin lands."

There are many other advances in agriculture which have yet to be applied on a large scale. The identification of necessary trace elements and their incorporation into fertilizers and feeds have opened vast areas to cultivation and husbandry in Australia and elsewhere. Selective breeding of plants and animals has permitted the development of species with superior hardiness and increased yields, in some cases multiplied them by a large factor. In the greater part of the world such work has hardly begun. Advances in animal health and nutrition have permitted the mass production of milk and eggs in indoor conditioners on a scale which was unimaginable a few years ago—the city of Los Angeles is now an important and efficient dairy area. . . . Herbicides increase yields, pesticides prevent losses from rodents, insects, and fungi—in many underdeveloped countries one-quarter of the crops is lost before it reaches the consumer. Certain methods of preservation of foods by radiation have just been approved by the Food and Drug Administration. Control of weather by seeding clouds for rain, speeding cloud formation by heating lakes by atomic energy, desalinization of brackish water by various methods are entering the realm of practical feasibility.

Powerful though these methods of "classical" agriculture are, I believe that they will, within the lifetime of most present inhabitants of this planet, be left far behind as methods of food production. The general public is still unaware of some new developments, their promise, and the extent of the means likely to be expended in the next decade in bringing the results of research to practical application. Large scale manufacture of food from petrochemicals started during World War II, when the Germans manufactured synthetic fats to feed forced labor groups. . . . During the fifties, little or no work was done in this field, but recently a number of the largest international oil companies have again become actively interested, and pilot plants are now in operation. . . . While the promise of abundant and cheap atomic power, widely heralded for the morrow in the more immediate postwar period, has shown itself slow to be realized, abundant and cheap atomic power is coming, and it may well be that oil will be increasingly a raw material for food and plastics rather than a fuel.

As a potential source of food production, photosynthesis can be used much more efficiently in algae than in higher plants. With proper mineral fertilization and with the proper rate of removal of the finished products, one square meter may serve to support algae production sufficient to feed a man. . . . Interplanetary travel of long duration and the organization of distant stations require not only recycling of oxygen and waste water; they necessitate the fabrication of food and its integration into the recycling of oxygen, water, and excreta. Over the next two decades, an increasing fraction of the several billion dollars which the United States and the Soviet Union will spend every year for space travel is going to be channelled into life support systems. . . . [W]e may have in space exploration . . . the technological equivalent of war—without the corresponding losses in men and in resources. The usable "fall-out" of such research is likely to be enormous. Certainly if economical harnessing of photosynthesis—through biological units or directly—can be realized under the hostile interplanetary, lunar, or martian conditions, it should become relatively easy to put it into effect on earth. All this is no longer science fiction. It is as much of a reality as the federal income tax. Obviously, a breakthrough in this field could for centuries altogether remove food as a limiting factor to population growth.

I hope I have said enough to show how dangerous it may turn out to be for the population problem to have been linked so closely to food as a number of writers have done. These have generally been conservationists and social scientists rather than agricultural or nutritional scientists, concerned—rightly—with the effects of crowding which they had observed. At the same time, not sure that the public and governments would agree with them that there was cause for concern—and action—based on these grounds, they have turned to the threat of a worldwide shortage of food as an easily understood, imperative reason for large scale limitation of births. Had they consulted nutritionists, agriculturists, and chemists, they might have chosen a more appropriate battle ground. For if we can feed an ever-increasing number of people—even if we feed them as badly as many of our contemporaries are fed—their argument fails. . . .

There is of course, another good reason for not tying population control to food: it is that this tie eliminates from contention rich countries—and in particular surplus countries such as ours. Our population is increasing faster than it ever has; our major nutrition problem is overweight, our major agricultural problem is our ever-mounting excess production. Does anyone seriously believe this means that we have no population problem? Our housing problems, our traffic problem, the insufficiency of the number of our hospitals, of community recreation facilities, our pollution problems are all facets of our population problem. . . .

. . . We need a population policy and we need it soon, for the United States as well as for the world at large, not because we cannot step up food production, but because we believe, like Plato and Aristotle, in trying for excellence rather than in rejoicing in numbers. Excellent human subjects will not be produced without abundance of cultural as well as material resources. We are likely to run out of copper before we run out of food, of paper before we run out of copper. We are short even in this country now of housing, of hospitals, and of educational institutions. Needs are, of course, infinitely more acute in most other areas of the world. Is it not more sensible to focus on these unmet needs, which are present for all to see, than to argue from inaccurate projections which furthermore do not support the unnecessary argument?

WHAT IS A 'DEMOGRAPHIC EXPLOSION'?

Translation from the CURRENT DIGEST OF THE SOVIET PRESS, published weekly at Columbia University by the Joint Committee on Slavic Studies, appointed by the American Council of Learned Societies and the Social Science Research Council. Copyright © 1966, the Joint Committee on Slavic Studies. Reprinted by permission.

1 Why does Guzevaty think there is a population problem in the developing countries?
2 To what extent does the author accept the Malthusian theory?
3 What is the major difference between those who accept Malthus' main thesis and the Marxist scientists?

A few days ago Literaturnaya gazeta published an interesting article by Prof. B. Ts. Urlanis, "Is There a Population Problem?" The article's chief merit is that its general direction is against a dogmatic, simplified view of population problems. Although economics and sociology are now advancing in our country, there is still some tendency to regard demographic [population] questions as not quite scientific and deserving attention only on the negative plane, in criticizing Malthusianism. Yet population problems do exist, and to underestimate them is to weaken our economic, political and ideological efforts.

At the second world conference on population problems, which discussed some 500 reports that had been submitted in advance, no one denied that the accelerated growth of the world's population creates definite problems that cannot be ignored. . . . It is well known that a water shortage is making itself increasingly felt in many huge cities and industrial areas of the world. Of course one cannot believe that these cities and areas will be left entirely without water as the population goes on growing; rapidly developing science and technology are helping to find new sources of water. At the same time, there is no basis for the opposite conclusion, that the problem does not exist at all.

Many of the countries of Asia, Africa and Latin America are experiencing particularly grave economic difficulties in connection with accelerated population growth. . . .

Before gaining independence, the colonies and semicolonies had a moderate or low population increase, since the high birth rate typical of these countries was counterbalanced by a high mortality rate. Hunger, poverty and unsanitary living conditions caused the spread of all kinds of grave diseases.

With elimination of the colonial regime, the emancipated countries obtained the possibility of taking measures, in the course of state construction, to improve sanitary conditions and the system of health services. These measures, and also the employment of effective new means against epidemics, sharply reduced the death rate (on Ceylon, for example, mortality dropped 40% in three years of successful struggle against malaria). This decline in the death rate, while the birth rate remained high, caused a sharp increase in population.

Of course, a high population increase is not in itself a calamity, as the Malthusians claim. In favorable social conditions, with a sufficient volume of capital investment, an increase in population, far from hindering economic and cultural development, has a stimulating effect upon it. After all, people, working people, constitute the chief productive force of society.

The trouble is that the developing countries have inherited from colonialism a backward economy with conservative forms of land ownership and land use and primitive farming technology. In these circumstances, with acute shortages of capital and skilled labor, the population growth rate has begun to exceed the production growth rate, particularly the rate of growth of agricultural production. . . .

In other words, *rapid population growth creates serious economic difficulties in many developing countries. Not, however, because an imaginary Malthusian "universal natural law" is operating, but because of the general economic backwardness of these countries, resulting from historically transient social-economic causes.*

The governments of many states have officially adopted, together with economic development plans, "family planning programs" aimed at reducing the birth rate. Such programs have been adopted by the governments of India, Pakistan, Ceylon, the United Arab Republic, Tunisia, Turkey, Chile and several other countries. It should be emphasized that these "programs" by no means involve legislative restriction on the size of families, any encroachment on the right of parents to have as many children as they wish. The "programs" as a rule provide for measures to spread knowledge of marital hygiene and to popularize birth-control methods. . . .

. . . The supporters of a Malthusian approach to population problems consider birth-control measures the *principal means* of overcoming all the economic difficulties of the developing countries and deny the *primary role* of social-economic transformations. Marxist scientists, on the other hand, pointed out that without *radical social-economic transformations* all attempts to regulate the birth rate will fail and will not solve economic problems fundamentally, since the dynamics of the birth rate depend on the social-economic conditions of society's life, and not vice versa.

QUESTIONS FOR CLOSER STUDY

1 Can it be said that the article in *U.S. News & World Report* assumes that the agricultural revolution is almost over, whereas Jean Mayer insists that it has barely begun? Why?

2 What is the main area of disagreement between Guzevaty and Dr. Chun?

3 To what extent might Jean Mayer's article answer the criticisms of Ya. Guzevaty?

4 Which is more important—how much is produced or the distribution of what is produced?

5 On the basis of the evidence contained in the readings how would you answer the question "Can Mass Starvation Be Prevented"?

CHAPTER 12

WHO
WILL BURY
WHOM?

In 1917, following the assumption of power in Russia by a small band of revolutionary Marxists, the debate between those who supported communism and those who supported capitalism was transformed into a genuine competition. Having created the Soviet Union, the communists could no longer merely criticize and theorize—they now had to perform. In the same fashion, the defenders of capitalism had to reconsider their indictment of communism as an "impractical theory."

The two economic systems have competed now for over 50 years. But the contest for popular support goes on.

Backers of capitalism point to the higher standard of living in the United States, while partisans of communism cite the Soviet Union's greater rate of industrial growth. Economists in each country, in their attempts to make out a case for their way of life, use statistical measures such as gross national product (GNP)—a country's total output of goods and services. Such statistics are a valuable source of information. However, they are so difficult to interpret that they have done little to settle the ideological dispute.

The readings for this chapter compare the capitalist and communist economies—insofar as they are represented by the United States and the Soviet Union. The readings illustrate some of the problems that trouble economists when they try to use statistical data. They also offer some evidence from which we can try to judge the merits of the two economic systems.

The first reading is from the translated remarks of former Soviet Premier Nikita S. Khrushchev, who, while visiting the United States in September 1959, agreed to answer questions following an address to a National Press Club luncheon in Washington, D.C. He was asked to explain what he had meant by his famous challenge, "We will bury you."

The second reading is from *Soviet Economic Power,* by U.S. economist Robert W. Campbell. In this brief extract from his book, published in 1960, Campbell explains some of the difficulties in making economic comparisons between the two countries. He gives detailed examples of how Soviet production statistics are computed.

The third reading is translated from an article, "The Soviet Economy and American Experts," that appeared in *Pravda,* a leading Soviet daily newspaper, on May 26, 1967. The author, V. Smolyansky, also is an economist. He argues that the Soviet economy is continuing its rapid growth.

The fourth reading, from a 1965 memorandum by the U.S. Department of State, insists that the Soviets are losing the race to overtake the United States.

The last reading is from an article by N. Smelyakov, Soviet

210

Deputy Minister for Foreign Trade, which appeared in a 1967 issue of the Soviet literary journal *Literaturnaya gazeta*. The author, who has traveled extensively in the United States, candidly criticizes the backward Soviet highway system. Although the article does not directly compare productivity, it does hint at a likely Soviet effort to close an important gap in the race to pass the United States.

WE WILL BURY YOU!

Abridged from KHRUSHCHEV IN AMERICA. Copyright © 1960 by Crosscurrents Press.

1 What did Khrushchev mean when he said, "We will bury you"?
2 How does Khrushchev describe the history of the change from one social system to another?
3 Do you think that Khrushchev looks forward to a long period of coexistence? Why or why not?

QUESTION: It is frequently attributed to you, Mr. Khrushchev, that at a diplomatic reception [in November 1956, in Moscow] you said that you would bury us. If you didn't say it, you could deny it; and if you did say it, could you please explain what you meant?

KHRUSHCHEV: There is only a small section of the American people in this hall. My life would be too short to bury every one of you if this were to occur to me. I did speak about it, but my statement has been deliberately misconstrued. It was not a question of any physical burial of anyone at any time but of how the social system changes in the course of the historical progress of society. Every educated person knows that there is now more than one social system in the world. The various states, the various peoples have different systems. The social system changes as society develops. There was the feudal system. It was superseded by capitalism. Capitalism was more progressive than feudalism. Capitalism created better conditions than feudalism for the development of the productive forces. But capitalism engendered irreconcilable contradictions.

As it outlives itself, every system gives birth to its successors. Capitalism, as Marx, Engels and Lenin have proved, will be succeeded by communism. We believe in that. Many of you do not. But among you, too, there are people who believe in that.

At the reception concerned, I said that in the course of historical progress and in the historical sense, capitalism would be buried and communism would come to replace capitalism. You will say that this is out of the question. But then the feudal lords burned at the stake those who fought against feudalism and yet capitalism won out. Capitalism fights against communism. I am convinced that the winner will be communism, a social system which creates better conditions for the development of a country's productive forces, enables every individual to prove his worth and guarantees complete freedom for society, for every member of society. You may disagree with me. I disagree with you. What are we to do, then? We must coexist. Live on under capitalism, and we will build communism. . . . [T]he brief history of our Soviet state does not speak in favor of capitalism. What place did Russia hold for economic development before the Revolution? She was backward and illiterate. And now we have a powerful economy, our science and culture are highly developed.

PERFORMANCE OF THE SOVIET ECONOMY: GROWTH

Abridged from "Performance of the Soviet Economy: Growth" from SOVIET ECONOMIC POWER by Robert W. Campbell. Copyright © 1960 by Robert W. Campbell. Reprinted by permission of the author and the publisher, Houghton Mifflin Co.

1 Does Campbell think that Soviet production statistics are incorrect? that Soviet economists deliberately lie? Why or why not?
2 What evidence does the author give to show that "double-counting" exaggerates the growth of Soviet industrial output?
3 How does the author show the relationship between price changes and the value of industrial output?

The Russians claim that their economy has grown much faster than ours. They further claim that this differential in rates of growth is inevitable, and as a result sooner or later they will overtake and then surpass the capitalist part of the world in terms of economic power. . . . [I]t is now generally agreed among economists working on these problems that the Soviet economy has grown faster than ours, even when the Soviet claims are discounted considerably. Whether or not they can overtake us, and if so, how long it is likely to take obviously depends on just what the differential in the rate of growth for their economy and for ours has been in the past, and is likely to be in the future. . . .

The official statistics computed and published by the Soviet government claim that over the period 1929-56 the average annual rate of growth of Soviet GNP has been 9.8 per cent per year. (. . .[T]he figure for the United States for the same period was 2.9 per cent per year.) This is so much above what other countries have achieved in comparable stages of industrialization that it appears on the face of it fantastic, impossible. Knowing that Soviet statisticians have proclaimed that "statistics are a weapon in the class war" Western economists have suspected that these figures are somehow falsified or biased. . . . This is not to say that the Soviet statistics are simply made up out of thin air. Soviet planners and economists must have accurate statistics for their own planning and administrative work, and it is the opinion of most Western economists that they do not keep two sets of figures—one for their own use and one to be published for the confusion of foreigners. Indeed this would really be almost an impossibility. . . .

. . . Some of the difficulties of assessing Soviet economic growth can be illustrated by examination of one concrete example, namely, the measurement of the growth of Soviet industrial output. Industrial output is one of the major and at the same time the most rapidly growing component of Soviet gross national product. . . .

The Russians claim that industrial output was twenty-one times larger in 1955 than it was in 1928 . . . [but there] are . . . deficiencies in the way the Soviet statisticians compute their industrial output index, which make it a very inaccurate measure.

1. First of all they measure the growth of industrial output with an index of *gross industrial output*. That is, in any year total output of industry is figured by first determining the value of output of every industrial enterprise, and then adding these together. These annual totals are then compared with each other to get the index.

Such a procedure involves double-counting of much of the output of industry, since the output of some of the factories is consumed in other factories in the same year to make other parts of industrial output. For example, most of the coke produced by some industrial plants is used up immediately in the blast furnaces that produce pig iron. It is obvious that the value of the pig iron is going to include the value of the coke used to produce it; i.e., the price of a ton of pig iron covers not only the labor used in operating the blast furnace but also the cost of the coke burned up in the process. If the value of output of the coke plant and the value of output of the blast furnace are added together, the value of the coke is counted twice. In GNP calculations, of course, this double-counting must be eliminated. What we are concerned with here, however, is not the absolute size of the real output of industry in a given year, but rather its size relative to output in some other year. And the use of gross output to measure growth of industrial output will not *necessarily* introduce an error. If the percentage of industrial output consumed within industry does not change from year to year, then the . . . rate of growth for gross industrial production will be identical with . . . [that] for net industrial output.

But it is possible for the ratio of gross output to net output to change over time. One way this can happen is through organizational changes. Imagine, for instance, a large machinery factory which combines many successive processes in the manufacture of machinery. Pig iron may be turned into castings in its foundry; the castings may then be passed on to a machining shop where they are finished, and then on to an assembly shop where they are assembled into the final product. Another part of the plant may take simple raw materials and make the bolts, screws, and so on that are used in assembling the machines. The factory may even have its own power plant which provides the electric power for the other parts of the plant. The output of this machinery plant would be measured by the total value of goods it finished and sold to other enterprises in the economy.

Imagine that now, without changing any of the processes or the number of workers or the amount of output, the plant is split into five separate units—a foundry, a machining shop, an electric plant, a bolt factory, and the assembly plant. The whole complex works just as before, and the only difference is that since each of the former shops is now an independent enterprise each sells its output to the other parts of the plant. What is the output of this collection of plants now? If one follows the Soviet procedure of determining the value of output of each enterprise, and adds these together, the total output will obviously be much larger than before. The output of the assembly plant remains the same as the entire complex before it was split up, but there would now be added to it the output of the four newly separated enterprises.

Has output really increased? Obviously not, but if one simply looks at the figures on gross output, computed by the same rule each year, it appears that there has been an increase in output. And the increase in output would obviously be quite large in the case we have postulated. . . .

It should be mentioned, of course, that such changes can also take place in the opposite direction, when formerly independent enterprises are merged, or when there is a decrease in specialization. But most observers think that the trend has been mostly the other way in the Soviet economy. There are two good reasons for this. The first is that along with the growth of the scale of output, nearly always comes specialization, leading to a larger number of stages in the processing. The second is that there is a great institutional bias favoring splits and opposing mergers in the Soviet economy. . . .

2. Another influence which exaggerates the Soviet measure of industrial growth has been the failure to correct adequately for changes in the price level. . . . Imagine, for instance, that a tractor plant puts out 5,000 tractors in a given year and that the price per tractor is 10,000 rubles. The total output of the plant would then be 50 million rubles. If in the next year it again produces 5,000 tractors, but the price has risen to 12,000 rubles the value of its output that year would be 60 million rubles. But clearly there has been no increase in real output; the rise from 50 million to 60 million rubles reflects only the price change. Obviously to measure output in terms of rubles, it is necessary to use the same prices in both years. By and large the Soviet statisticians have tried to use "constant" prices. . . . Until recently the prices that existed in 1926-27 were used as "constant prices." . . . But in an economy like that of the Soviet Union, which is being transformed from a backward to a modern

one at a very fast rate, there inevitably arose many situations when a 1926-27 price was required for a completely new product, one that had not been produced anywhere in the Soviet Union in 1926-27. Faced with this problem, there were several things the statisticians could do. The simplest way out would be to give up and just use the present price. This was done at times and because there was a rapid inflation, new output was counted in at a value above the true 1926-27 level of prices. A better way would be to try to estimate how much it would have cost to produce this product in 1926-27 if it had been produced then, or to correct the present price to the 1926-27 level by noting how much the prices of similar products had increased in the intervening years. These latter two expedients might have been perfectly all right. But given the constant pressure from above for increased output, the people at the plant level were naturally biased in favor of setting as high a "1926-27 price" on these products as they thought they could get away with. The rapid inflation made the high prices seem more credible. . . .

Just how important a bias this has been in the Soviet index no one knows. It is thought to be fairly important in the machinery and chemical industries, for example, where there is a constant introduction of new products.

**THE SOVIET ECONOMY
AND AMERICAN 'EXPERTS'**

Translation from the CURRENT DI-
GEST OF THE SOVIET PRESS, published weekly at Columbia University by the Joint Committee
on Slavic Studies, appointed by
the American Council of Learned
Societies and the Social Science
Research Council. Copyright ©
1967, the Joint Committee on
Slavic Studies. Reprinted by
permission.

1 Why do you think Smolyansky uses percentages when comparing the growth of U.S. and Soviet industrial output?
2 Do you think Smolyansky is accurate in his defense of the New Economic Policy? Why or why not?

The times when the opponents of the new world declared socialism "illegitimate" have long since receded into oblivion. Now even the most malicious foes of the U.S.S.R. are forced to acknowledge the vitality and strength of the new social system. While acknowledging this, imperialist propaganda at the same time is striving at any cost to dampen the effect of the tremendous successes achieved by our people in the 50 years of Soviet rule and to deny the immeasurable advantages, proved by life, of socialism over capitalism. As if this were not enough, the ideologists of the bourgeoisie are trying to implant the idea that the socialist economic system is supposedly "sliding" and "evolving" in the direction of capitalism.

. . . To give their arguments a semblance of authenticity, the adversaries of communism pass off the fortuitous for the natural, the specific for the general. In their theses and conclusions they attempt to shift to the socialist economy the operation of economic forces inherent in capitalism.

Such, in particular, is the methodology of the experts of the U.S. Congress in publishing their latest [1966] five-volume collection, "New Directions in the Soviet Economy."

1.—Repeating in every key the story of the Soviet economy's "permanent failure" and making use of some figures from a recent short-term slowdown in the rate of its development, American experts draw an analogy between the U.S.S.R. national economy of recent years and the U.S. crisis economy of the 1930s. This is really, as they say, placing the disease onto the healthy party!

Today every schoolboy knows that crises are inherent only in a capitalist economy; they lead the latter to a decline in output, a decrease in the volume of domestic and foreign trade, unemployment and a sharp drop in the working people's living standard. Thus, in connection with the crisis of 1929 [beginning of the Great Depression], the United States by the beginning of the 1930s were set back 28 years in coal production, 36 years in pig-iron production, 31 years in steel production and about 30 years in the volume of foreign trade.

Compare this with the economic status the Soviet Union attained in 1966, as opposed, say, to 1958 . . . . Coal output totaled 585,000,000 tons in our country, as opposed to 493,000,000 tons in 1958; the figures for steel were 96,900,000 tons and 54,900,000 tons respectively; electric power output totaled 545,000,000,000 kwh. [kilowatt-hours] as opposed to 235,000,000,000 kwh. . . . .

. . . In four months this year [1967] the volume of industrial output in our country increased by 10.5%, and in the U.S.A. by only 2.2%. Steel output has risen 6% in our country, and in the United States it has declined by 5%. Electric power output increased by 5.8% in the U.S.A., and by 10% in the U.S.S.R.

Soviet people note with pride that in the first quarter of 1967 our metallurgy attained a level that assures an output of more than 100,000,000 tons of steel a year. It becomes clear that the Soviet Union has marched confidently ahead during these years, and by no means has experienced . . . "crises" . . . .

Whereas the average annual rate of growth of industrial output in the U.S.S.R. during the seven-year plan (1959-1965) was equal to 9.1%, the U.S.A. approached this growth rate only in certain years. Consequently, the higher efficiency of the socialist economy manifests itself in consistently higher rates of economic growth.

A fact remains a fact: Crises are organically inherent not to socialism but to capitalism. In the U.S.S.R. and the other socialist [communist] countries, under normal—i.e., peacetime—conditions of sociopolitical and economic development, every successive year has been higher than any previous year in the level of output. In the countries of capital, on the other hand, output moves forward cyclically, through periodic crises and recessions. Thus, according to economists' calculations, in the period between wars (1918-1939), the United States, due to crises and recessions, incurred losses approximately equal to 2.5 years' output at annual average for that period, or more than 12% of the total industrial output for those years. And since World War II the U.S.A. has lost for the same reason more than a year's output, equal in absolute terms to all the losses by industry in the period between the wars.

We recall that in the period of U.S. industrialization (1860-1913) the rate of its economic development amounted to about 5% annually, while in the Soviet Union in the First Five-Year Plan [1928-1932] it reached 19.2%; in the Second [1933-1937] 17%; and in three years [1938-1940] of the Third Five-Year Plan, 13.2%. The superiority of socialism in terms of growth rates will be no less evident if even a later period is taken. . . .

In the present five-year period the volume of industrial output in the U.S.S.R. will increase by about 50%. Even in a favorable period, the American economy has achieved such a growth, accord-

ing to official U.S. statistics, only in a time span twice as long—
1955-1965.

It is typical that the higher percentage rise in the American
economy last year (the gross national product increased by 5.5%)
to a considerable extent is accounted for by the boom engendered
by the war in Vietnam. Military expenditures in the U.S.A. in the
new fiscal year will reach a record figure—$75,500,000,000 as opposed
to $13,000,000,000 in 1949-1950 and $22,500,000,000 in 1950-1951,
i.e. at the height of the Korean War, which brought about, as is well
known, a feverish rise in war production and in the profits of the
largest American monopolies. . . .

2.—The experts of the American Congress endeavor to present in a false light not only the present stage but all of Soviet economic history. They try to convince the public at large, for example,
that the New Economic Policy [Soviet economic reconstruction program of the 1920's] was a deviation from the normal path of socialist
development; the NEP was supposedly the result of "a crisis of the
system."

Discussions of NEP serve the American experts as a kind of
prologue to an interpretation of the Soviet economy today. They
perform a "subtle" ideological move—they build a bridge between
NEP and the economic reform [which emphasizes profits and strict
cost accounting by factory managers] currently being carried out
in the U.S.S.R., characterizing both as a "return to capitalism" or,
more precisely, as a steady movement toward "market socialism."

But it is well known that NEP was a new political and
economic strategy and tactic applicable to the conditions of that
time. The heart of the matter lay chiefly in the fact that the surplus-
appropriation system was replaced by a tax in kind and the task of
establishing a commodity link between socialist industry and the
individual peasant economy in conditions of a temporary permission for private initiative on a limited scale was solved.

At the same time, the New Economic Policy was marked by
the introduction of commercial marketing principles as the norm
for economic management in the socialist sector. NEP provided
the conditions for the victory of socialism in the U.S.S.R.

V. I. Lenin [founder of the Soviet Union] pointed out: "The
New Economic Policy does not change the single state economic plan

and does not transcend its framework, but it changes the approach to its implementation."

**U.S.S.R. FALTERS IN
ECONOMIC GROWTH RACE
WITH THE UNITED STATES**

"U.S.S.R. Falters in Economic
Growth Race with the United
States" (November 1965) from
Department of State Bulletin.

1 Why does the author think the Soviet Union found it more expensive to develop a space program than to improve and increase its industrial output?
2 How does the author demonstrate that the Soviet GNP is overtaking that of the United States?
3 What reasons are given for the slowdown in Soviet economic growth?

The [annual] rate of growth of Soviet GNP has slowed down from about 6½ percent in the 1950's to about 4½ percent in the 1960's. . . .

The slowdown in Soviet economic growth is the result of many factors, but from the vantage point of mid-1965 a few key points may be singled out for attention:

(1) The expansion of defense expenditures after 1958 preempted a large share of the high-quality resources most needed to modernize industry and agriculture. The new military programs proved to be voracious consumers of the best scientific and engineering talent, the most costly and complex machinery, and the newest alloys and other high-cost materials.

(2) Linked with the first factor was the failure of agriculture to provide a reliable domestic source of food and raw materials for industry. . . . The near-disastrous harvest of 1963 dramatized the failure of the Soviet leadership in dealing with agricultural problems; on this occasion about 11 million metric tons . . . of wheat and flour had to be imported from the capitalistic West at a cost of almost $1 billion. . . .

(3) The Soviet economy in the 1950's benefited greatly by adopting new technology and manufacturing processes from the West at relatively little cost. But when the Soviet leaders had to solve

their own problems—for example, in the space field—they could no longer bypass the costly research stage by leaning on the West . . . .

(4) . . . The growth in the Soviet economy in the 1950's was powered by a rapid step-up in investment, whereas in the 1960's the planners have had to settle for smaller percentage increases in investment—and in overall economic growth. Moreover, the Soviet leaders have tried to compensate for the decreased rate of growth in investment by keeping old capacity in operation. . . .

Even though the Soviet economy is faltering in its growth race with the U.S., a reminder is needed about the basic economic strength of the U.S.S.R. The present rate of growth is quite respectable for a modern industrial nation. At the current average rate of growth of 4½ percent, Soviet GNP would double in 16 years. . . .

An interesting aspect of U.S. performance in the growth race is that even in industrial production the U.S. has matched the U.S.S.R. stride for stride in percentage growth since 1961. Of course, in absolute terms U.S. industrial production is growing much more rapidly—more than double the Soviet growth. . . .

Agriculture accounts for something less than one-third of Soviet GNP and industry for somewhat more than one-third. The remaining one-third is a diverse group of products and services which includes construction, transportation, trade, communications, education, health, and government administration. A large segment of this miscellaneous third rises or falls according to the fortunes of agriculture and industry. . . .

During the new five-year period, 1966-70, the factors that have dictated a slowdown in Soviet economic growth are likely to persist. Attempts to restore rates of growth in industry would be largely at the expense of agriculture and perhaps defense, and in turn new large-scale investment in agriculture would reduce the extent to which industry could be modernized. . . .

. . . Suppose that over the next five years the U.S.S.R. is able to halt the declining trend in the rate of growth which has developed in recent years and maintains for example a rate of 4½ percent, while the U.S. economy continues to grow at a rate of 4 percent. Soviet GNP in 1970 would still be about half that of the U.S., and Soviet per capita GNP would be about 43 percent of the U.S. level. Moreover, since the Soviet consumer's share in GNP is unlikely to rise, Soviet per capita consumption would remain little better than 30 percent of U.S. per capita consumption.

**AN EXPENSIVE ROAD
IS THE CHEAPEST**

Translation from the CURRENT DI-GEST OF THE SOVIET PRESS, pub-lished weekly at Columbia Uni-versity by the Joint Committee on Slavic Studies, appointed by the American Council of Learned Societies and the Social Science Research Council. Copyright © 1967, the Joint Committee on Slavic Studies. Reprinted by permission.

1 Do you agree with Smelyakov that the United States has no bad roads?
2 Are you surprised that the author openly criticizes his country? Why or why not?
3 Why do you think he wrote this article?

It is said that it is hard to be objective in discussing another country if you love your own boundlessly. To my mind, this is untrue. Real devotion to one's homeland in fact requires maximum depths in studying foreign experience and accuracy in describing it. . . .

America is the captive of the automobile. Cars, new and shabby, shining and rusty, speed along its first-class roads. . . .

In the U.S.A. today, according to American statistics, on the average, every family has an automobile. . . . The total number of motor vehicles exceeds 83,000,000, including 70,000,000 passenger cars. According to estimates made by American specialists, in 1975 there will be 114,000,000 motor vehicles in the U.S.A. . . .

. . . [N]early all adults know how to turn the wheel. Few of them, true, can repair a car, or fix even a minor defect. But there are special services for this. Every highway is lined with a palisade of repair and filling stations. Here one can find everything for the automobile and its passenger. The cars are washed, their windows wiped, their tires checked and, if necessary, pumped. At the driver's request, his automobile is raised by hydraulic hoist to have a look at the working parts—preventive inspection never hurts. . . .

A highway without such services, even if the surface is in perfect condition and the road signs are good, is like a boundless desert in which the driver is left to his own resources. Take, for example, Moscow's splendid new Belt Highway. Its shores are unpopulated. Whatever happens to you, you must see to it by yourself! Are there many filling stations along this motor artery in the capital? Do you often come across repair stations there? A place to wash your hands, have a bite, or drink a cup of coffee? All these things are castles in the air. It is almost impossible to buy a guidebook, or find out anything. Nor is it easy to make a telephone call or send a telegram. Yet this road is in the capital! It was built quite recently; all the demands made on a modern highway could have been taken into consideration.

Americans say that the automobile has created roads. There are no bad roads in the U.S.A. Satisfactory roads are replaced by good roads; good by excellent ones; excellent ones by first-class, extremely up-to-date expressways. . . . Even in out-of-the-way places one sees good roads with hard surfaces. . . .

In the U.S.A. the roads are adapted to the automobile. In our country, however, the automobile is adapted to the poor quality of the roads. When the question of the birth of the Soviet automobile was being decided, some people even expressed doubt: Did we need such a thing at all? Automobiles require good roads, they said, . . . assuming that bad roads were intrinsic to Russia and would remain with us forever.

. . . [O]vertones of these assertions can be heard even to-day. . . .

Many people, of course, realize very well the importance of good roads; but their construction requires enormous capital invest-ments, and we have many other primary tasks. Yet this is the only correct path—to build real, up-to-date highways. All expenses, no matter how great, will be compensated a hundred times over. It is no accident that American advertisements depict roads with dollars moving along down them—symbols of the advantages and profita-bility to be derived from their construction.

A glance at a U.S. road atlas will disclose a picture aston-ishing to anyone who knows even a little about how roads are built and maintained and how much they cost. One is struck by the den-sity of the network and the straight lines of even local roads.

The speed of road construction in America is amazing. . . . This is the result of a high level of integrated—really integrated—mechanization, up-to-date technology, splendid material supply and the specialization of the people engaged in road construction.

The quality of the cement and all the materials without exception is of no little importance. . . . Roads are built to last lifetimes. They must do without capital repairs for decades. . . .

Studying . . . America, I saw, of course, quite a bit there that is fit to be consigned to the dustbin of history. But much of the exceedingly rich experience of that country can and must be used in our own. . . .

. . . Rural roads . . . are of special importance in our country. Imagine a collective or state farm where any field could be reached by highway in any weather. The losses in grain crops alone would be reduced 25% to 30% if they could be conveyed along asphalt roads directly from the fields to the elevators.

What about all the other advantages! The transport of people, various types of machinery, chemicals and fertilizers to the fields? What about communications with the city? What about the daily lives of the rural population? One can hardly enumerate all the advantages an extensive network of good highways would bring to agriculture. They would eliminate many problems connected with . . . the rapid delivery of foodstuffs, building materials, industrial commodities and other types of freight. . . .

The economic importance of highways can hardly be over-estimated. There is good reason to regard them as a factor of primary importance to the state. Any neglect with regard to their construction is an expensive mistake.

Of course, there is a time for everything. In the Soviet Union there is a plan of action for the development of every branch of the national economy, including highway construction. Now, however, when the foundations for new automobile plants are being laid and old ones are being expanded, the question of highway construction acquires special importance.

QUESTIONS FOR CLOSER STUDY

1 Which readings do you think are the most objective? Why?

2 What arguments not used by the authors of the readings can you think of to support the U.S. economic system? the Soviet economic system?

3 Do you think 50 years is long enough to show which system is the best? Why or why not?

4 How do you account for the difference in presentation and content when you compare Smelyakov's article with Smolyansky's article?

5 What are some of the weaknesses in using GNP as a measure of economic performance when comparing two countries?

6 Where can you find reasonably accurate and comparable economic production figures for the United States and the Soviet Union?

7 Do Soviet statistics automatically eliminate any possibility for accurately comparing capitalism and communism?

4235

44389